Modern Antiquities:

Comprising

Sketches of Early Buffalo and the Great Lakes

Also Sketches of Alaska

Modern Antiquities:

Comprising

Sketches of Early Buffalo and the Great Lakes

Also Sketches of Alaska

by Barton Atkins

Originally Published by
The Courier Company, Printers and Binders
Buffalo, New York
1898

Media Hatchery
Orchard Park

All text and illustrations in this publication are in the public domain and were obtained from the Library of Congress. All other text, design, and formatting are
© 2020 by William C. Even — Media Hatchery.

All rights reserved.

ISBN: 978-0-9971276-7-6 (Paperback Edition)

Library of Congress Control Number: 2020923503

Front cover illustration:
Map of Erie County, New York: from actual surveys—1854.
Library of Congress, Geography and Map Division.

Printed and bound in the United States of America
First Printing 2020

Published by Media Hatchery
P. O. Box 554
Orchard Park, NY 14127

MediaHatchery.com

DEDICATION.

To my son, David, who has absolutely no idea how much I appreciate him spending more evenings than I am certain he cares to count, helping me proofread this document. Of course, if you do find any mistakes, they're his fault.

It had been many years since I read him a bedtime story. I do miss those days.

— W. Even

The Walk-in-the-Water—1818.

EXPLANATION.

THIS WRITING IS IN MANNER PROVINCIAL. LITERARY MERIT IS NOT ESSAYED, AND FOR ITS DEMERITS NO APOLOGY IS OFFERED.

COPYRIGHTED, 1898,
BY BARTON ATKINS

MODERN ANTIQUITIES.

CHAPTER I.

At the burning of Buffalo in 1813 its earlier records were destroyed. From recollections of early residents, and from letters of early travelers, written hence, were constructed a history of the early trading-post and the subsequent village of New Amsterdam.

The immediate ancestors of the writer were early residents of the locality, and of its legendary lore he was invested with a liberal share, which, together with the records of the reconstructed village of Buffalo, form a basis for the claim that such history as is herein presented is the truth of it.

About the year 1790 is the date when came the first white settler, and who erected the first building where now is the populous city of Buffalo. The historic pioneer was a Hollander and an Indian trader, named Cornelius Winne, from Fishkill on the Hudson. Thus, in reality, it was the Hollander, Winne, and not Ellicott, the agent of Hollanders, who was the founder of Buffalo.

The commercial importance of Winne's domain was of slow growth during the remainder of the century. In 1791 Col. Thomas Proctor, an emissary of the Secretary of War, came to Western New York to treat with the Seneca Indians, and at the trading-post he found Winne, and a negro, called "Black Joe," the only signs of civilization.

Four years later, in 1795, Capt. Daniel Dobbins journeyed from "Genesee Country" to Presque Isle (Erie), and at the mouth of Buffalo Creek he rested for a day with Winne and Black Joe, who were then partners in trade with the Indians. Captain Dobbins found the population of Winne's colony doubled, by the addition of Johnston, the British interpreter, and the Dutchman, Middaugh. Capt. Daniel Dobbins was not only an early pioneer among savage life, but a fighting patriot as well. Prior to the war of 1812 he was sailing the waters of Lake Erie, master of the schooner *Salina* and when war came was prompt to join the navy, and in the battle of Lake Erie was commander of the *Ohio*, one of Perry's fighting fleet. All honor to the memory of Capt. Daniel Dobbins!

Three years subsequent to the visit of Captain Dobbins, in 1798, Albert Brisbane visited the trading-post "Lake Erie," and found its population further increased. "There were five or six log-houses. In one John Palmer kept a tavern, in one lived Asa Ransom and family, in another James Robbins, a blacksmith, and in a double house lived Johnston, the interpreter, and Middaugh, with his son-in-law, a man named Ezekiah Lane, who was a cooper." Middaugh had squatted over the creek, about opposite the present foot of Main street, where he lived an Indian trader until his death, in 1825. Lane was a resident in Buffalo until his death, in 1865—a centenarian.

Mr. Brisbane found that Winne and Black Joe had sought other pastures—Winne in Canada, and Joe on the Cattaraugus reservation, where he lived many years, dying at an advanced age. Joe Hodge had lived among the Indians a long time, spoke their language fluently, and had an Indian family. Was said to have escaped from slavery when a boy, and took refuge with the Senecas.

In the year 1800, dating from Fort Niagara, Rev. Elkanah Holmes, a missionary from New York, wrote to his principals as follows:

> I then took leave of him (Farmer's Brother) and went to a village of white people at the mouth of the Buffaloe. While there, where I made my home during my visit to the Senecas, I preached to the whites seven or eight times. They never had but one sermon preached there before.

Historians date Mr. Holmes' first appearance in Western New York in 1801, and to him they give credit of preaching the first sermon in Buffalo, It appears authoritively that he was there in 1800, and preached seven or eight times, and that there was one sermon preached there before his. Mr. Holmes did not name the preacher of the first sermon, an omission fatal to a complete record of the preaching of the Gospel in Buffalo.

The letter here quoted, together with a speech made to Mr. Holmes by Farmer's Brother, and another by Red Jacket, the chief Sachems of the Seneca Nation, were published in the *New York Missionary Magazine* of December, 1800. Herein is the first republication of the letter and speeches.*

At this time Mr. Holmes found five or six families at the trading-post, but does not mention any names. He went to New York in the fall of 1800, but returned the following year a missionary to the Senecas, remaining with them on the Buffalo Creek Reservation until 1812.

In the meantime the title to the lands adjacent to Lake Erie became vested in the Holland Land Company, and in

* See Appendix.

1799, their agent, Joseph Ellicott, appeared on the scene with a corps of surveyors, and in the following year he mapped a town site which he named New Amsterdam. The eligible location of the town site drew hither many prospectors, and the town increased in population rapidly.

The first mechanics, other than jack-knife carpenters, to ply their trades in the town, were James Robbins, the blacksmith, and Ezekiel Lane, the cooper. The first tavern was opened by one Skinner, in 1794. He is spoken of by travelers before Palmer, who probably succeeded Skinner. The first civil official was Asa Ransom, who was appointed justice of the peace by Governor George Clinton, in 1801.

And with the coming of a court of justice occurred the first murder in the town. An Indian, called Stiff-Arm George, stabbed to death John Hewett, in front of Palmer's tavern. The murderer was arrested and tried at Canandaigua. In his defense Red Jacket addressed the jury, citing cases of white men killing Indians and not punished therefor, as a reason for the discharge of the prisoner. The culprit was convicted, however, and subsequently pardoned by the Governor on condition that he leave and remain without the state, a condition faithfully complied with. The industry of hanging Indians in Buffalo was not ripe at that early period.

In 1803, David Reese, a blacksmith, came to the Senecas, making their knives and hoes, repairing their guns, etc. For Red Jacket he made a tomahawk, which was unsatisfactory to the big Indian, he casting it on the ground with the utterance, "No good." Then Reese was furnished with a pattern of a weapon desired by Red Jacket, and, when making, Reese was admonished to strictly follow the model, which instruction was rigidly observed, and the illustrious savage had a tomahawk without a hole therein for a handle, and this is why he ever after called Reese

"Damfool." Reese's shop stood on the northeast corner of Washington and Seneca streets, a frame building painted red, one of three not burned by the British, and where the bodies of the slain villagers were gathered and prepared for burial. The little red shop continued to adorn that now picturesque corner until about 1820.

A school-house was erected in 1803—a house of hewed timber—on Cayuga street (Pearl), west side, below Swan.

The first physician to locate in New Amsterdam was Dr. Cyrenius Chapin, and there he continued to reside until his death, in 1838. Dr. Chapin was active on the frontier during the war of 1812, and valorous in defense of Buffalo in troublous times. He is recalled as a tall, spare and gray-visaged man, wrapped in a long cloak of blue cloth.

As Indian Agent, Judge Erastus Granger called Dr. Chapin to attend Red Jacket in his illness. The original bill presented to Judge Granger for this service is possessed by the writer, dated December, 1806.

The bill of Dr. Chapin reads as follows:

ERASTUS GRANGER, Esq., Dr.
To CYRENIUS CHAPIN.

For medical attention, and for med. delivered to Red Jacket, Nov. 5, 1806:

Two Emetics,	4s.
Croton Oil Pills,	6s.
Sol. Tartar Emetic,	3s.
Spice and Opium Plaster,	4s.
Pills of Croton Oil,	.1s.
	£0.18s.0

Item Second.

19-Call,	.2s.
Cathartic,	2s.
Sol. of Glauber-salts,	3s.
Emetic of Powdered Ipecac,	4s.
Pills of Croton Oil,	8s.
	£0.19s.0
	£1.17s.0

Received Payment, Buffalo Creek,
    Dec'r 14th, 1806.   Signed duplicates,
      EBEN'R WALDEN.   CYRENIUS CHAPIN.

Some of the doses thus prescribed have been known to kill a horse, but Red Jacket survived the treatment twenty-four years, a pleasing assurance that his monument in Forest Lawn was not erected in vain.

The first regular mail came from Canandaigua on horseback, in 1804. Then a post-office was established, and Erastus Granger appointed postmaster.

The first lot devoted to burial purpose in the settlement was the one now the northeast corner of Washington and Exchange streets. There interments were made until the "Village Burial Ground" was established—where now is the City and County Hall—in 1808. The first interment in the village ground was the body of a stranger, who died suddenly at Barker's tavern, formerly Pomeroy's. No lots were sold in the village plot; burial permits were granted by the trustees.

In 1815, the famous Seneca chief, Farmer's Brother, was buried there with military honors. In later life this native warrior was friendly and loyal to the whites, and to the Government of the United States. In earlier life he led the war party which committed the ghastly massacre of Britons at Devil's Hole, on the Niagara.

At the commencement of the war of 1812, the schooner *Connecticut*, an American vessel, when anchored off the mouth of Buffalo Creek, was captured by a British party from Fort Erie, the first hostile act of the war on the frontier. Soon thereafter two British vessels were anchored near shore, under the guns of Fort Erie. Lieutenant Elliott, of the navy, then at Buffalo, organized an expedition to cut out the Britishers under cover of night, and his success was complete, for which Congress voted that heroic officer a sword. Subsequently Elliott admitted that the sagacious Farmer's Brother pointed out to him the feasibility of his expedition to capture the British vessels, one of which had a valuable cargo of furs, brought down from Lake Huron.

Interments continued in the village plot until 1836, the wife of Judge Samuel Wilkeson being the last one, excepting the body of Dr. Cyrenius Chapin, which was buried there by special permit, in 1838. Dr. Chapin's grave was directly beneath the present Church street entrance to the city hall. The remains of those interred in the old village ground were removed to an inclosed plot in Forest Lawn, in 1850.

David Mather was a settler in New Amsterdam in 1806. Then the hamlet consisted of sixteen houses, eight of which were on Main street, three on Seneca, two on Pearl, and three on the Terrace. There were two stores, one on the southeast corner of Main and Seneca streets, kept by Vincent Grant, and the store of Samuel Pratt, on Crow street (Exchange), which then extended only from Main to Washington street. In a wing of his dwelling, corner of Main and Crow streets, Louis Le Couteulx had a drug store, the first in Buffalo. Where now is the Mansion House, John Crow kept a tavern.

The first lawyer to locate in New Amsterdam was Ebenezer Walden, in 1806. And in 1811 Mrs. Walden presided at the first piano sounded in Buffalo. The first judge for Buffalo was Samuel Tupper, appointed in 1805 by Gov. George Clinton. Judge Tupper resided on the southwest corner of Main and Tupper streets. His dwelling was destroyed in the burning of the village in 1813. After the war he erected a larger house on the site, where it remained until removed to the west side of Main street, below Allen, and where it still stands, a relic of village days.

The first street passenger line in Buffalo was established by Moses Baker, in 1825—a line of stages to and from Black Rock.

CHAPTER II.

THE preceding chapter relates to the coming of the first white settler to "Buffalo Creek," and the establishment of the trading-post, "Lake Erie," and of the subsequent village of "New Amsterdam," and of events there occurring down to the year 1807. At that period the settlers of the place persisted in calling it Buffalo, in accord with the official name of its post-office and the customs district. But not until 1826 were the Dutch appellations of the streets officially renounced and the present names substituted.

In 1808 an act of the legislature made Buffalo the county seat of Niagara County, the Holland Company donating lots, on which were erected a court-house and jail. The court-house, a wooden structure, was located on the present line of Washington street, directly fronting the present Public Library building. The jail was built of stone, and stood where now is the old Darrow block, on Washington street, opposite the Mooney-Brisbane building. These improvements added prestige to the town; settlers came, and its advance was rapid.

The first court of record was held in 1808, at Landon's tavern, Augustus Porter, Judge, William Stewart, District Attorney, Louis Le Couteulx, Clerk, and Asa Ransom, Sheriff. Upon this court were four attendant lawyers, Ebenezer Walden, John Root and Jonas Harrison, of Buffalo, and Bates Cook, of Lewiston. The records of the court went the way of all other records of early Buffalo—up in smoke in the conflagration of 1813, but in some manner it has been preserved to history that at this session four men were indicted and tried for stealing a cow!

The first brick building erected in the town of Buffalo was by William Hodge, Sen., in 1806, on the lot now 1358 Main street. The bricks for the building were manufactured by Mr. Hodge on the lot now occupied by the Bapst building, corner of Main street and Glenwood avenue. The second brick structure in the town was erected on the lot now the northeast corner of Exchange and Washington streets, in 1810, by Benjamin Caryl, Juba Storrs and Samuel Pratt, Jr.

The first newspaper for Buffalo was the *Gazette* published by Smith H. and Hezekiah Salisbury, in 1811. Copies of this publication are preserved in the Buffalo Library.

The first brewer known to Buffalo was Joseph Webb. In 1811 he advertised his brewery in the columns of the *Gazette*.

In 1811 the first church organization in Buffalo was formed—"The First Congregational and Presbyterian Church"—numbering twenty-nine members, as follows:

James B. Hyde,	Jabez Goodell,
Rusha Hyde,	Nancy Hull,
Samuel Atkins,	Ruth Foster,
Anna Atkins,	Keziah Cotton,
John J. Seeley,	Nancy Mather,
Elizabeth Seeley,	Keziah Holt,
Stephen Franklin,	Sally Haddock,
Sarah Franklin,	Sophia Bull,
Amos Callender,	Henry Woodworth,
Rebecca Callender,	Sophia Gillett,
Nathaniel Sill,	Betsy Atkins,
Keziah Sill,	Mary Holbrook,
Comfort Landon,	Louis Curtiss,
Esther Pratt,	Nancy Harvey,
Sarah Hoisington.	

For about four years the society retained its original title, when it was changed to "The First Presbyterian Church Society," a name still retained. The vicissitudes of war interrupted their meetings for fully three years. The Rev. Thaddeus Osgood was their first pastor. In May, 1816, in a building on the northeast corner of Main and Huron streets, erected for a carpenter shop, the Rev. Miles P. Squier was installed pastor. Their old church, which gave place to the Erie County Bank building, was erected in 1827. Its foundation stones were dug when constructing the canal at Porter avenue.

The first butcher to open a meat market in Buffalo was Gilman Folsom, in 1808. His location was on the lot since occupied for a like purpose for half a century by Arnold Weppner, on Main street, below Chippewa. Folsom's slaughter-house was in the rear, on Pearl street. In 1811 a war-cloud darkened the land. To frontier communities remote from the centers of population it was of much concern. When war came it brought appalling disaster to the village of Buffalo, its inhabitants being compelled to flee from the flames of their burning homes in mid-winter to seek shelter in adjacent settlements. Their village, with the exception of three buildings, was burned to ashes.

Recently was published in a local newspaper a conservative account of the burning and of the events leading thereto, which is new reading. The article is hereto appended:

> The story of the burning of Buffalo eighty-three years ago has been told many times, but almost always from the point of view of the dwellers in the two villages where the city now stands. The men of Buffalo and Black Rock were defending their own firesides, and Buffalonians are apt to think of them and their families as the only sufferers. It will be interesting to read the story as seen by those who rallied from the surrounding country to aid in defense of Buffalo when its destruction was threatened.
>
> When General Wilkinson retired in 1813 to lower Lake Ontario, he left the force on the Niagara in command of General McClure, who made his headquarters on the Canadian side, at Fort George, where the doughty General issued flaming proclamations, and when abandoning that position committed the needless cruelty of burning the adjacent village, and turning helpless families out into winter's cold and snow. The inhuman act brought condign punishment on the American frontier. Then McClure moved his headquarters to Buffalo. The British, fired with the spirit of revenge, at once undertook reprisals. The whole country-side, up to Tonawanda Creek, was swept by redcoats and their savages. During the three weeks following the burning of Newark, six American villages were burned, with all the scattered homes the avengers could find. The whole countryside was a waste. General McClure called upon the men of Genesee, Niagara and Chautauqua counties to come to the defense of Buffalo, and then went to Batavia, where he arrived on December 22d, and there he gave up the command to General Hall, who hurried on all the troops he could to Buffalo, which he reached December 25th, and did the best he could to repel the invaders.
>
> The tale has often been told how small detachments of American raw militia were one after another thrown against the enemy in the darkness at Conjockety Creek, and were in turn demoralized, many

scattering through the wood in flight; how the British succeeded in landing at Black Rock; how the enemy marched up from the Conjockety, dispersing such resistance as they met. General Hall sounded a retreat, hoping to make a stand at Buffalo, but this was impossible. Only a few soldiers rallied for a future defense. Then followed a scene which passes description. The few roads were thronged with a motley crowd of soldiers and citizens and Seneca Indians, all hurrying as fast as possible from the British and their savage allies. For a day or two the country roads resembled a general May-day moving, but with terror blanching every face.

Such was the effect of the needless destruction of the Canadian village by General McClure on his evacuation of Fort George, and who then and there disgraced the uniform of an American soldier by so doing. What if the villagers were insulting to their invaders? They were belligerents in time of war, and their indignities should have been overlooked, and innocent women and children not subjected to inhuman treatment in order to appease the wrath of an officer in command. A true soldier would have shrunk from such action.

Until the spring of 1814, but few of the fugitive villagers returned to re-establish their homes, and most of these with pluck only as a resource. The *Gazette* of May 14 announced that activity prevailed in rebuilding, and that the county clerk's office could be found at the house of Major Miller, at Cold Spring, that the post-office was at the house of Judge Granger, and that the collector's office had returned from Batavia. Samuel Wilkeson had returned from the army, and on Niagara, near Main street, he erected a house, and still another on Main, near Genesee street. The latter was his family residence until the completion of his mansion on Niagara Square, in 1825.

This house, since construction, has been occupied continuously by the Wilkeson family. Miss Louise Wilkeson, a granddaughter of Judge Samuel Wilkeson, its present occupant, has there resided from her birth. The house is of much historic interest. Therein important meetings were held by prominent, influential citizens, when ways were discussed and means were provided to advance the interests of Buffalo. There Gov. Dewitt Clinton and Canal Commissioner Myron Holly met in consultation with citizens of Buffalo on matters important, and which, promoted by the master mind of Judge Wilkeson, were consummated to the advantage and glory of Buffalo. On the opening of the Erie Canal, Judge Wilkeson was chairman of the celebration committee, and on their return from their eastern trip a grand reception was held at the Wilkeson house, where the returned committee was greeted and congratulated by the leading residents of Buffalo, and of the country surrounding.

Robert Cameron Rogers, in his story, "Johnny Wedderburn," locates a scene at the Wilkeson mansion, he naming it "Wedderburn House." The story is not drawn from family history, but his description of the house and grounds is perfect:

But the uproar never seems to break in upon or dispel the air of complete repose which surround the old mansion. The very dust appears to settle with a certain deference over the garden and through the branches of the elm trees, which stand like drowsy sentinels just within the yard. The Wedderburn House is like a half-hour stolen for meditation out of a busy day. It is a little Mecca in the midst of the work-a-day world, into which you may turn to meditate awhile on remote and quiet themes, and even, as the moslem leaves his shoes without the mosque, bid the questions and anxieties of life await you at the gate. Within the house is the same atmosphere of rest, tinged, you might say, with sadness. The shadow of some lingering sadness, softened and mellowed by time, seems mingled with the quiet of the dusky rooms. As you tread through the long hall, the soft, odd-patterned rugs hush the footfall into silence. The old-fashioned furni-

THE WILKESON MANSION.

ture meets your gaze, seeming to say softly, "We have been long in the family, and have memories."

Together with its central location, and the historic interest connected with the house and grounds, their purchase and preservation by the city is a subject worthy of consideration. The result would be a joy to future generations, and a debt of honor canceled which Buffalo owes to the memory of Samuel Wilkeson, the father of the city—the founder of its commercial greatness.

In the spring of 1813 the first execution in Buffalo took place. Two soldiers were shot for desertion, at the camp on Flint Hill. A like tragedy occurred the following year, when five soldiers were placed in kneeling posture to be shot for desertion, one of whom was a young man under twenty years of age. The muskets handed to the men ordered to fire at him were charged with blank cartridge, and his life was his own. This tragedy, overlooked by Generals Brown, Scott and Ripley, took place where is now the junction of Seventh and Carolina streets.

The first execution by civil authority in Buffalo was in 1815, when James Peters and Charles Thompson were hanged for the murder of James Burba. The victim lived on the river-side, below Black Rock, and because he objected to the trespass upon his premises by Thompson and Peters, they shot him. On this occasion the gallows was erected on the Terrace near Swan street.

In December, 1819, for the second time a gallows was erected in Buffalo. John Godfrey was hanged for killing a soldier in the garrison at Fort Niagara. The recruit was dilatory in obeying an order of Corporal Godfrey, and thereupon he was promptly shot, and for which the corporal was promptly hanged, and then the scales of Justice balanced even.

The first three years of the reconstruction of the village were uneventful, when important events stimulated the villagers to greater activity. The construction of the Erie Canal, then in progress, and the advent and success of a steamboat on Lake Erie, were incentives to emigration, and the ensuing decade was largely eventful to Buffalo.

In 1813 an act incorporating the village was passed by the legislature, but the exigencies of war prevented organization. Another act of incorporation was passed in 1816, when an organization was effected, with Oliver Forward, Samuel Wilkeson, Charles Townsend, Ebenezer Walden, Heman B. Potter and Jonas Harrison as trustees.

A paper written in 1847, by the late Judge George W. Clinton, is an interesting chapter of village history, from which the following is extracted:

> On the 6th of May, 1816, the freeholders and inhabitants met at the house of Gaius Kibbe, innkeeper. Of the trustees, Samuel Wilkeson, Oliver Forward, Charles Townsend and Jonas Harrison were present. The meeting chose J. E. Chaplin, Clerk, Josiah Trowbridge, Treasurer, Moses Baker, Collector, and Reuben B. Heacock, John Haddock and Caleb Russell, Fire Wardens. At a subsequent meeting, on the 11th of November, 1816, they voted the first tax ever imposed in Buffalo village—a tax of $1,400, to be apportioned according to the assessment roll of the town of Buffalo for that year.

On the 7th of March, 1817, the trustees organized a fire company, and appointed the following named to constitute it:

Sylvanus Marvin,	Horatio L. Fobes,
Stephen K. Grosvenor,	Joseph Lawton,
William Murray,	Jonathan R. Brown,
Jonathan E. Chaplin,	Azariah Fuller, Jr.,
Dan Bristol,	William B. Goodrich,
Gorham Chapin,	Nathaniel Goodrich,
John Fobes,	William Dorrington,
John B. Hicks,	Welcome Wood.

At this meeting the trustees passed a resolution, rather arbitrarily, "that it be the duty of Vincent Grant, Gilman Folsom and Amos Callender to protect property from plunder whenever a fire takes place in this village."

In May, 1823, was passed the first ordinance forbiding domestic animals the freedom of the town, but the cows and pigs refused to observe the law for many years thereafter by roaming at will.

On the 6th of August, 1825, Lorin Pierce was appointed village sexton, an office he held persistently for fifty years thereafter.

On December 16, 1824, the second fire company was organized. Among the members were:

Guy H. Goodrich,	Abner Bryant,
Thaddeus Weed,	Martin Daley,
Ebenezer Johnson,	John A. Lazelle,
George Coit,	George B. Gleason,
John Scott,	George B. Webster,
William Hollister,	Robert Bush,
Nathaniel Wilgus,	Joseph Dart,
Theodore Coburn,	E. D. Efner,
Hiram Johnson.	

In August, 1831, a tax of $3,000 was imposed for the purpose of constructing reservoirs and the purchase of fire engines. Two thousand dollars was paid for a fire engine and 200 feet of hose. Then a third fire company was organized. Two engine houses were built and a third one ordered, and another fire engine contracted for. Such were the youthful days of Buffalo's now unsurpassed fire department.

The police department was organized by a provision of the city charter; the village trustees neglecting such precaution further than to appoint a "watch," at the request of the residents of the "Triangle," situated between Main and Canal streets and the canal. John Benson, Michael Benson and William Cornwall were appointed to guard that locality—Buffalo's first police authorized by the corporation.

Not until near the close of the village era was Buffalo furnished with a sidewalk other than what Mother Earth provided. An order to construct sidewalks on Main street, from Crow to Swan street, was ordered in 1829, "with brick or smooth flagging," at the expense of the owners of fronting property—the west side to be sixteen feet in width, and but fourteen feet on the east side, and both sides provided with a rail on the outer edge.

Prior to 1845, the east side of Main street below Seneca was of but little account. The east side, called "Cheapside," was "in the swim." As late as 1846 the corner of Exchange and Main streets was occupied by the residence of Louis Le Couteulx, upon a hill ten feet above the present grade. The lot was inclosed by a stone wall, eight feet high above the sidewalk. On the Main and Exchange street fronts there were openings in the wall, where steps led up to a gate at the top of the ground entrance to the house. From the corner of Exchange street half-way to Seneca street was vacant property. In 1843 William Carland came from Boston. Adjoining the Le Couteulx lot on the north he erected Gothic Hall, the building now occupied by that combustible merchant, Salem LeValley. Mr. Carland's enterprise was scoffed at by the merchants of "Cheapside"—that his building would be out of the line of business and travel. However, his fine structure was the incentive to the immediate improvement of that side of the street, above and below, when at once it became what it has ever since remained—the bustling side.

During the Presidential campaign of 1844 the Whigs, in honor of their candidate, Henry Clay, erected on the upper corner of Main and Exchange streets a massive ashen column, twenty feet high, surmounted by a golden ball, in circumference equal to a flour barrel.

The first settlement of Buffalo was in the vicinity of the Terrace Liberty Pole. The double log-house of Middaugh and Lane, sold to Judge Barker in 1808, was the first exclusive dwelling erected. No contracts for the sale of lands in New Amsterdam were entered into by the Holland Company until November, 1804, when six were made on the first day. One of these was inner lot No. 1, to John Crow, who erected and kept a tavern upon it, and a public house has been maintained thereon continuously since, known as the Mansion House. In 1810, this lot, with its improvements, was sold to Joseph Landon for $140. The census of 1810 gave the village a population of 355 white inhabitants.

The year 1816 gave to Buffalo four brick buildings, two of which became famous—the court-house for its noted lawyers, and for its many noted criminal trials, among which were the convicted murderers, John Godfrey, the three Thayers, Dibdell Holt, John Davis, John Johnson, McElroy, Shorter, Knickerbocker, and the acute Gaffney—all hanged, from Davis down, in the old jail yard. Holt was the victim of the last public execution in Buffalo. A noted trial in the old court-house was that of the illustrious forger, Benjamin Rathbun, in 1838.

Once upon a time, Millard Fillmore, a respected Buffalo lawyer, who, with the rest of mankind, did not then suspect that he was destined to be President of the United States, addressed the jury in an important land case, tried before Judge Mullett in the old courthouse. The close of

Mr. Fillmore's address was an appeal to the jury, when he stated that "they all knew him, and therefore were aware that statements he had made to them were the facts of the case, else he would not have made them." Then Mr. Fillmore took a seat next to the late Judge Talcott, then a lawyer at the bar. The opposing counsel, Gen. George P. Barker then arose to make his address. General Barker opened his argument by protesting against the eminent counsel for the plaintiffs making his personal character "the right bower of his argument." Mr. Fillmore was curious: "Right bower—right bower—what's that?" whispered the future President. "Biggest knave in the pack," said Talcott, and without a change of countenance.

The Eagle Tavern acquired fame for good cheer, superior viands and entertainment. Among its guests, from time to time, have been Presidents of the nation. Governors, statesmen, and foreign potentates when making pilgrimages to the Falls. When the American Hotel burned in 1865, the remaining portion of the old Eagle Tavern was destroyed, and on its site was erected the stores, 416 and 418 Main street.

The first landlord of the Eagle Tavern was its constructor, Gaius Kibbe. In the early twenties Kibbe was succeeded by Benjamin Rathbun, who there flourished until the fall of 1836. Rathbun was succeeded by E. A. Huntley, and he for a time by I. R. Harrington, but its prestige had departed, overshadowed by the adjoining American Hotel.

A third structure was the residence of Judge Walden, located on Main street, where now stands the south end of J. N. Adam's line of stores, between Eagle and Clinton streets. Mr. Walden disposed of the property in 1823 to Bela D. Coe, the resident proprietor of the Albany and Buffalo line of stages, who occupied the residence until about 1839, when W. A. Moseley took possession, until sold to the McArthurs, during the forties. The McArthurs added to the premises by inclosing the then vacant space to Eagle street. For many years thereafter it was "McArthurs' Garden," having a building within the inclosure for exhibitions, with stage and audience room. Here Gen. Tom Thumb was first exhibited in Buffalo by P. T. Barnum. Subsequently, in 1851, a panorama presented scenes on the Sacramento River where gold was being panned out; the exhibitor spread the California fever when pointing to a locality on the canvas, and saying: "On that bar I worked six weeks, averaging a little over two hundred dollars a day." The corner below, where stands the Hotel Iroquois, was then vacant. Usually, in summer, a circus tent was pitched in this lot. It was here that Dan Rice, in 1858, exhibited his educated mules for the first time in Buffalo. Then upon the corner was erected the St. James Hotel, opened by E. L. Hodges, and then the Young Men's Association purchased and occupied the property about 1865, and then the fated Richmond Hotel, and then—the big wigwam, the Iroquois.

CHAPTER III.

At this period, 1820, no water craft larger than a bateau could enter Buffalo Creek from the lake, and the construction of a harbor was the leading question considered by the villagers. For the extension of the Erie Canal to Buffalo a harbor was indispensable, and a harbor its people were determined to have.

Application for a survey of the creek was made, and an act passed authorizing such a survey. A survey was made, and then a public meeting appointed Charles Townsend a delegate to Albany to obtain legislative aid. The state would loan a sum of money to be applied to building a harbor at Buffalo provided security was furnished. Oliver Forward, Charles Townsend, A. H. Tracy, H. B. Potter, E. F. Norton, Ebenezer Johnson, Ebenezer Walden, Jonas Harrison and John G. Camp associated and applied for a loan. An act was passed authorizing a loan to above-named citizens of Buffalo to the amount of $12,000, to be secured by bond and mortgage in double the amount. But the outcome was that all but Charles Townsend and Oliver Forward declined to bond themselves. Then the prospect of Buffalo village becoming a commercial city was cast in gloom. The termination of the canal at Black Rock was influentially advocated, and the practicability, even the possibility, of constructing a permanent structure at the mouth of Buffalo Creek was seriously questioned. At this juncture came forth a Moses, who opened the way through the wilderness. The benefactor was Judge Samuel Wilkeson, who, in connection with Judge Charles Townsend, Judge Oliver Forward and George Coit, gave the required security, each executing their individual bond and mortgage in the sum of $6,000. They obtained $12,000 from the state to be expended in making a harbor at Buffalo, the state reserving the right to take the work when completed and cancel the bonds, all dependent upon its stability. The building of a pier into the open lake was an experiment,— no such work had been attempted. An engineer for superintendent was imported from the sea-board, and the work commenced during the summer of 1821. Judge Wilkeson was prosecuting his private business. Judge Forward was a senator at Albany, while Judge Townsend, not in robust health, watched the action of the superintendent, making himself acquainted with his plans and management. After a time it became manifest that the imported expert was improvident, if not incompetent, that he was not an economist sufficient to complete the work with the money available. A consultation resulted in the discharge of the superintendent, and obtaining the consent of Judge Wilkeson to neglect his private affairs and assume the management of the work.

The great energy of Judge Wilkeson was evinced in the accomplishment of the first day of his management, three cribs being constructed, placed and partially filled with stone. For the want of adequate means of excavation and other appliances the work was prosecuted under many difficulties; incessant rain and rough water was a hindrance that could not be obviated, and during the month of September, when the cribs placed were filled with stone, the work was suspended for the season.

In his writings Judge Wilkeson was generous with praises of his faithful assistants in harbor work. Of Sloan and Olmstead, the stone boatmen, he writes interestingly:

> Those only who have experienced the difficulties in making improvements in a new country with inadequate facilities, can appreciate the worth of such men. James Sloan was a salt boatman on the Niagara river in 1807. During the war he was a lake sailor, was of the party who cut out the brig *Adams* from under the guns of Fort Erie, and was commander of the ammunition boat at the siege of that fort. He was industrious, faithful and honest.

In after life Capt. James Sloan resided at Black Rock, engaged in boating on the Niagara, an honored citizen, until his death, about 1857. Most old citizens will recall his sturdy character and quiet demeanor.

In his writing of Olmstead and his achievements, a heroic character and a thrilling incident are added to local annals:

> N. K. Olmstead was a man of unusual muscular power. The severe labor he performed on harbor work, perhaps no man in the country could equal. He lived in Buffalo when the village was burned by the British, and his home and property were destroyed. When peace was declared he declined to be a party to the contract, remaining alert to make reprisal while on the river. Managing to obtain a load of military supplies to transport from Chippewa to Fort Erie, which included two kegs of specie, he landed on the American shore and hid the money. He then left the frontier, but returned to Buffalo in 1819. When on harbor work he at times went to the Canada shore for boatloads of stone, and on such an occasion was arrested and placed in a boat to be taken to Chippewa. The boat had a small skiff in tow, in

which was a single paddle. When nearing Chippewa he leaped into the skiff, cut its fastening, and took to the rapid current, where his captors declined his pursuit. By extraordinary exertion he landed on Grass Island. Observing a boat putting out from Chippewa, he again braved the rapids, and managed to make Porter's mill-race. A less active and powerful man would have been swept over the falls. The next day he resumed harbor work.

The question of the terminus of the Erie Canal was greatly agitating the community, when Oliver Forward was selected as the master mind to represent the interests of Buffalo in the legislature, where he maintained a conspicuous position and accomplished the great object of his mission, favorable legislation for Buffalo.

Judge Charles Townsend was one of those pioneers who will ever be remembered as identified with the settlement and progress of Buffalo, and who in an eminent degree contributed to create and advance its business and commercial interests.

Judge Samuel Wilkeson is gratefully remembered and more generally known from his identification with the history and prosperity of Buffalo. He was an extraordinary man, of strong mind, great energy and perseverance, possessing great public spirit and active enterprise.

These men gave to Buffalo a harbor at a time opportune. No harbor, no canal; no canal, no city. The harbor of 1822 was the harbinger of commercial greatness, fabulous in proportions, and, in view of the grand results, the most important consummation in the world of commerce.

The successful navigation of the Hudson and Delaware rivers by steam, led to its application for the navigation of Lake Erie. Early in the winter of 1817 the following named persons associated to construct a steamboat for Lake Erie: Joseph B. Stuart, Nathaniel Davis, Asa H. Curtis, Ralph Pratt, James Durant and John Meads, of Albany, and Robert McQueen, Samuel McCoon, Alexander McMuir and Noah Brown, of New York. Mr. McQueen, a machinist, built the engine, and Mr. Brown, a shipwright, constructed the hull. The engine was constructed in New York, and from Albany conveyed in wagons to the bank of the Niagara. The hull and boiler were built at Black Rock. Early in 1818 Mr. Brown laid the keel on the bank of the river, a short distance above the mouth of Conjockety Creek, in a ship-yard made historic by the building there of a portion of Commodore Perry's fleet five years previous, with which he fought and won his historic victory on Lake Erie. There, on May 28, 1818, was launched a boat with dimensions as follows: Length, 135 feet; width, 32 feet; depth, 8½ feet; tonnage, 338; carrying mainsail, foresail and foretopmast staysail. On the 25th day of August following, the steamboat *Walk-in-the-Water* departed from Black Rock on her first passage over the turbulent waters of Lake Erie, bound for Erie, Grand River, Cleveland, Sandusky and Detroit. Over this course the boat reached Detroit in 44 hours, developing a speed of seven and one-half miles per hour. When the steamboat essayed to stem the current of the Niagara, a scene picturesque and humiliating must have been presented. Fancy a steamboat, in order to make progress, calling to its aid a team of oxen, and then struggling at the end of a tow-line while the oxen on the beach were alike struggling under the incentive of an elongated ox-goad, and you have the picture! Such was the inauguration of steam navigation on the Great Lakes eighty years ago.

The elongated and hyphenated name of the original lake steamboat met unfavorable criticism, and the origin thereof partakes of the romantic. In 1807, when Robert

Fulton first steamed the *Clermont* up the Hudson, an Indian, standing on the bank, gazing silently at the boat stemming the current unaided by sails, finally exclaimed, "Walks in the water!" The denizen of the forest saw the boat ascend the stream unaided by visible power—by none known to him. He saw the paddle-wheel revolve, and conceived that when a paddle struck the surface of the water a step forward was taken. A grand conception of an untutored mind! Of course the boat walked in the water; what else? This intuitive estimate of the original steamboat sentimentally suggested a name for the first steam vessel on the lakes. But the unwieldy name met with adverse criticism, and was seldom applied—the boat having no compeer—"The Steamboat" being considered quite significant, and which was her usual appellation.

The steamboat continued to ply successfully between Black Rock and Detroit until November, 1821, when a violent storm of wind beached her a short distance above the mouth of Buffalo Creek. To the growing lake commerce of the village the loss of the boat was a serious matter, happening at its very doors, yet the calamity received but slight consideration from the local newspaper. As an exhibit of the progress of journalistic enterprise, the article devoted to the wrecking is interesting. Evidently the fate of passengers and crew was not considered of importance by the local writer. The following is his contribution:

> It is with regret that we have to announce that "The Steamboat" was beached about one hundred rods above the mouth of Buffalo Creek, and is so badly damaged that she cannot be repaired. The boat was heavily laden, and on her last trip for the season. We cannot learn whether she was insured or not.

But for a subsequent publication of the details furnished by a passenger on board, posterity would have been deprived of a thrilling romance, the last voyage of the *Walk-in-the-Water*. The narrative is pathetic, and unique in nautical description, reading as follows:

> On Wednesday, October 31st, at 4 o'clock P. M., "The Steamboat" left Black Rock on her regular trip to Detroit. The weather, though somewhat rainy, did not appear threatening. After proceeding a short distance up the lake she was struck by a severe squall, which continued to blow through the night with extreme severity. The lake became rough to a terrifying degree, and every wave seemed to threaten destruction to the boat and passengers. To proceed up the lake was impossible. To attempt to return to Black Rock amid the darkness and howling tempest would be certain destruction. She was then anchored, and for a time held fast. The casings in her cabins moved at every roll, and the creaking of her timbers was appalling. She commenced leaking, and her engine was devoted to the pumps, but the water increased to an alarming extent, and the wind increased to an alarming degree. The wind blew more violent as the night advanced, and it was discovered that she was dragging her anchors. The passengers were numerous, and many of them were ladies, whose fears and cries were truly heart-rending. In this scene of distress and danger, all the passengers feel the warmest gratitude to Captain Rogers for the prudence, coolness and intelligence with which he performed his duty. The boat was now at the mercy of the waves, until five o'clock in the morning, when she beached, and we all debarked.
>
> BUFFALO, November 6, 1821.

The advent of the steamboat on Lake Erie was thus announced by the local newspaper of Buffalo. Queer does it read at this period:

> The ladies and gentlemen of this village were yesterday gratified with an excursion on board the new and elegant steamboat *Walk-in-the-Water*, by the politeness of Dr. Stuart, one of the promoters. The boat left the bay, off Buffalo Creek, at 3 o'clock P. M., and proceeded off Point Abino, and returned at 7 o'clock. It is with much pride that

we can recommend this mode of travel to all who desire celerity. We hope the owners will reap a full harvest for their efforts to extend the usefulness of this invention, which ennobles American character.

The ennoblement of American character was all right, but that the boat was the harbinger of a vast commerce for Lake Erie, and of essential importance to local interests, evidently had not then dawned on Buffalo journalistic enterprise and "much pride."

The wreck of the hull of the steamboat was complete, but her machinery remained intact, and as she had been a financial success, it was determined to replace her by the building of a new hull. Then the citizens of Buffalo entered into correspondence with the builders, urging such construction at Buffalo, resulting in a promise to that effect if assurance be given that a channel would be provided for the boat out onto the lake when completed.

Early in January, 1822, Mr. Noah Brown, shipwright and builder of the original boat, came from New York to commence the construction, and first appeared at Black Rock, Buffalo people not being aware of his arrival until it was announced that the boat was to be built at Black Rock, and that the contracts for material were to be executed at the Mansion House that evening. Buffalonians were advised that Brown was instructed to build at Buffalo, with conditions equal, and were indignant at his hasty action in not having conferred with them before concluding to build at Black Rock. When evening came the lower rooms of the hotel were filled with indignant villagers to demand explanation from Mr. Brown, then in the house, and determined, if possible, to obtain a reversal of his decision in favor of Black Rock before contracts for the delivery of material were signed. The gentlemen from the river village were on hand to receive their contracts, and whatever was done must be done quickly. Judge Wilkeson was selected to first interview Mr. Brown. The Judge was unacquainted with the gentleman from New York, but there was no time for formalities. "Get the boat built here and we will sustain your action," were his instructions, and he then sought out the seclusion of Mr. Brown and proceeded to business.

In correspondence with the principals Judge Wilkeson was advised that if a bond was given that a channel would be constructed in time to meet the wants of the boat, Mr. Brown was instructed to build at Buffalo, and thereby was prepared for a pointed dialogue. It opened thus:

"Mr. Brown, why do you not build your boat here, pursuant to the promise of the company?" was the direct question put. With dignified tone and manner came the reply:

"Why, sir, I arrived in your village at an early hour, and concluded to occupy the morning in consulting the ship-carpenters at Black Rock, who worked for me in building the *Walk-in-the-Water*. While there I was told that your harbor project was a humbug, and if built here the boat could not get out into the lake. Besides, the timber contractors would not deliver timber here as cheaply as there, and that is the reason why I concluded to build at Black Rock."

Many older citizens will readily imagine the determined attitude of Judge Wilkeson at this critical moment. As usual in emergencies, he was equal to the occasion. His language was plain, and its directness sublime:

"Mr. Brown, our neighbors have done us injustice. Sir, we are prepared to make you this proposition: We will at once execute a bond to pay to your company $150 per day for each and every day the boat is detained for the want of a channel into the lake after the first day of May next. The bond will also stipulate that all required timber for construction will be furnished at a less cost than offered at Black Rock. We will at once place in your hands a sum of money, the same to be forfeited in case a sufficient bond is not immediately executed and to you delivered."

It was known that the agent was predisposed in favor of Black Rock, but the proposition squarely meeting his instructions, together with its earnest delivery, subdued the gentleman into meekness in his reply:

"Mr. Wilkeson, your proposition is quite satisfactory, and therefore I have no alternative but to accept it. My attorney, Mr. Moulton, will see that the documents are properly made out and executed."

The day following a bond was executed, receiving the signatures of nearly all responsible residents of the village, and a contract to furnish all required timber was taken by William A. Carpenter, and by him fulfilled. The boat was built on the bank of Buffalo creek, where now is Indiana street, and when completed was taken out on the lake by Captain William T. Miller, and returned without hindrance, and so continued to pass out and in for twelve years thereafter. The passing of the steamboat out and in from the lake doubled the value of all the landed property in the village and its surroundings. With the villagers it was a day of jubilee, and tradition says the majority did not disturb their beds until the dawn of the next day. The indomitable will and energy Judge Wilkeson displayed in the construction of the channel for the steamboat was the talk of the town for years after. He had labored with the workmen, often in water, and conformed to the rule governing the hours of labor, from daylight to evening twilight. With him it was a labor of love, he receiving no recompense for his service other than benefits received in general. The work performed was the excavation of a channel through a point of sand and gravel twenty yards wide, having an average height above water of seven feet, to a depth of nine feet below the water level. A modern dredge would make an easy and short job of it, but then only improvised implements for excavation below the surface of water were to be obtained, and of a nature most crude.

CHAPTER IV.

Public amusement for Buffalo villagers was first provided in 1820, when Mr. Charles, a ventriloquist, gave exhibitions in the court-house. Then a caravan, comprising an elephant, camel, lion, tiger, zebra, and a family of monkeys, were exhibited. Then came a show of wax figures, representing notables of Colony times. On Main below Clinton street was a theatre, where "King Richard" first appeared in Buffalo in the person of Mr. Maywood. And there Tom and Jerry appeared before their advent in a liquid state. In 1828 Mr. Lowell established a museum in the building now 242 Main street, he leasing the premises from Josiah Beardsley.

My earliest recollection of public entertainment was that of "Old Sickles' Show," which with me antedates the circus. During the decade of the thirties, a benevolent-faced, bald-pated old Yankee from Connecticut, named Sickles, made annual visits to Western New York exhibiting his puppet show, an entertainment designed to please the juveniles, who, with their grandmas, mammas and aunts, were his delighted audiences. Usually the show was given in the ball-room of the neighborhood tavern, where, from a wire stretched across the upper end of the room, draw-curtains were suspended, which, when drawn, an assemblage of puppets appeared, representing both sexes, and which, through their connection with invisible wires, would hold receptions, dance reels and minuets with precision, taking steps in time to the notes of an invisible violin. In addition to the puppets a series of tableaux were presented, ending with that of the "Babes in the Woods," a scene designed to bring sobs and tears from the child audiences. There was represented a lonely forest, the lost children lying on the ground in death's embrace, when would appear a family of robins, hopping and flitting about, gathering leaves, with which they covered the dead babes. The effect of this scene on sympathetic childhood is illustrated in a verse of Eliza Cook's "Address to the Robin":

> How my tiny heart throbbed with sorrowful heaves,
>   That kept choking my eyes and my breath,
> When I heard of thee spreading a shroud of green leaves
>   O'er the little ones lonely in death.

The original troupe of Negro Minstrels—"burnt cork artists"—was organized and first exhibited in Buffalo in the latter thirties, by Edwin Christy, a dock saloon-keeper. The industry was original with Christy, he taking inspiration from the performance of Dick Sliter and George Harrington, two town boys. Sliter was precocious as a jig dancer, while Harrington could beat time with his hands expertly. When about fifteen years of age, the boys would repair to the steamboat wharves and display their peculiar talent to admiring crowds, who would strew small coin around the feet of the dancer. At first the beaten jig time was a rapid patting on the fore thighs, called juba:

> Juba up and juba down,
> Juba all around the town, *ad finitum.*

Christy patronized the two boys, Harrington being his step-son, usually called George Christy, who would locate their exhibitions fronting or within his saloon. Christy was a fine ballad singer and a violinist, and in these accomplishments the step-son was his diligent student. With Sliter and Harrington the nucleus, by adding tambourine and banjo players, and an additional violinist, an exhibition troupe was constituted, and in a room over his saloon, Christy, as manager, gave daily and nightly his "Darkey Minstrel Show" to crowded houses, and from the first opening Christy's fortune was secure. From time to time additional talent was added, and "Christy's Minstrels" were widely famous in their portrayal of negro character, excentricity and extravaganza. Christy was progressive in taking his troupe to New York City, where he established them in permanent quarters, and where they continuously performed to crowded audiences, their manager eventually retiring with a fortune. Thus originated the "burnt-cork artists," so numerous for years thereafter.

Dick Sliter became the most diverse dancer in the world. In a match exhibition against John Diamond, he danced his Rattlesnake Jig one hour and five minutes without repeating a step. During his exhibition tour he traversed two continents. In London, in private exhibition, he jigged before an audience of royalty.

A ferry across to Fort Erie from the historic black rock, near Bird Island, existed at an early date, there being one reported by early voyagers in times of the Revolution. In 1800 one O'Neil operated it, until 1806, when Major Frederick Miller took charge, and in 1808 he gave over to Asa Stanard. In deference to the war the ferry was suspended in 1812 for a time, until 1814, when it was renewed by Lester Brace. Until 1821 Brace operated the ferry, when Major Donald Fraser became proprietor. The boats used were scows, propelled by sweeps, wielded by the strong arms of four skilled watermen.

In 1825 Lester Brace and Major Fraser built the horse-power boat, which they continued to operate until steam-power was adopted for the ferry by James Haggart, in 1840. In the construction of the Erie Canal in 1825, the old rock, which so long served as a ferry landing, was blasted away and the landing removed to where it remains, at the foot of Ferry street.

The old-time horse-boat was a curiosity of the period, it being the pioneer of its kind west of the Hudson river. When first operated it received liberal patronage from many curious to inspect its working. The machinery of the boat consisted of a horizontal tread wheel the width of the deck and placed even therewith, and having a system of cogs and gearing which turned the shaft holding the paddle wheels. The horses trod on either side, the driver between with whip in hand, with which he flayed the poor beasts while the boat was under way. When a boy, the writer often crossed the Niagara river on the horseboat, and, while pitying the poor horses, detested the man with the whip.

Major Donald Fraser was a valiant soldier of the war of 1812. He was on the staff of General Pike when that brave officer was killed at Toronto; was on the staff of General Brown at Chippewa and Lundy's Lane; aide to General

OLD FERRY LANDING.

Porter at Fort Erie, and captain of the horse-boat when there were no battles to fight. A brave man and a patriot was the Major, and withal a Scotchman, and as a Scotchman I am proud of him—as said Josh Billings of his ancestor who was a "phiddler."

In March, 1824, the lone steamboat on Lake Erie was thus advertised:

> The steamboat *Superior* will sail from Buffalo on or about the 20th day of April, next, if the lake is then clear of ice, making nine day trips during the season—the November trips dependent on the state of the weather. Passengers will be landed at Grand River, Cleveland and Sanduskly, unless prevented by stress of weather. If a trip should be made to the upper lakes during the season, due notice will be given. All shipments of merchandise on the boat will be at the risk of the owner or shipper thereof, and that the captain of the boat is to receive no freight unless shipped under such conditions.
>
> J. I. OSTRANDER,
> ALBANY, March 16, 1824.   Secretary.

During the decade of the twenties, village newspapers contained many unique advertisements, some of which were spiced with humor.

A dealer in pottery desired those indebted to him whose promises had matured, to make payment, "or new promises."

An advertiser, with absurd honesty, called attention of the owner to a green cotton umbrella left in his office.

H. S. Seymour dealt in lottery tickets. He graciously, by advertisement, notified "two young men, living somewhere in the town of Clarence, that their ticket purchased of him had drawn a prize of one thousand dollars, and that the cash was awaiting the rightful owners at his office."

An advertisement of Peter Colt makes the diversity of the present department stores ancient history: "Pork, whisky, cross-cut saws, buffalo robes, gin and feathers."

In connection with a general store, Pratt and Meech did a forwarding business. They were enabled to guarantee the delivery of goods from Albany "in the short space of twelve days." They offered for sale, "drugs, dye-stuffs, medicines, surgical instruments, leather, Indian blankets, rum, log-chains, groceries, salt, whisky and whitefish."

"For Sale—A negro servant girl," was the advertisement of Jonas Harrison.

In 1820 five young negro slaves were brought to Buffalo from Kentucky, the property of Mrs. Gen. Peter B. Porter. After filing a bond that they would be liberated at the age of twenty-one years, Mrs. Porter was permitted to hold her chattels.

Samuel Edsall called attention to his tannery and shoe-shop, situated "on the road to Black Rock, near the village of Buffalo," now the corner of Niagara and Mohawk streets.

For Sale—A lease of lot No. 4, Le Couteulx Block, opposite Cheapside. On the premises are two stores with rooms in the rear for dwellings, and space for family gardens. One dollar and fifty cents per foot front per annum.   Thomas Quigley.

The location is now 191 Main street.

A prominent hotel advertisement reads as follows:

E. Belden, proprietor of the Mansion House, respectfully informs the public that he has taken the old-established stage house at the south end of the village of Buffalo, long known as the Landon stand. The house is large and in complete repair. Its spacious piazzas furnish the most extensive, rich and varied prospects of land and water, overlooking Buffalo harbor, Niagara river. Fort Erie, the lake, and extensive landscapes on the American and Canadian shores. His extensive yards, gardens and shrubbery will furnish pleasant and refreshing retreat to ladies and gentlemen after the fatigues of travelling. Carriages with safe drivers and moderate fare will be furnished to men of business or parties of pleasure wishing to travel out of the usual stage routes. His stables and pastures are large and convenient. His house at all times will be supplied with the fruits of the season, and the best liquors and provisions the country affords; and he trusts that approved experience and punctual attendance and good servants will keep up the long-established character of the house, and give general satisfaction to the public.

BUFFALO, July, 1824.

CHAPTER V.

The year 1825 was largely eventful to the people of Buffalo. The celebration of the opening of the Erie Canal was an event of wide importance, reaching from the seaboard to the confines of Western civilization, with Buffalo the storm-center, as it were. Gov. Dewitt Clinton and staff came to Buffalo and, with a local committee, boarded the *Seneca Chief*, a boat constructed for the purpose, and made the passage of the canal to Albany. The departure of the boat was announced by the discharge of a 32-pounder. Other cannon were placed on the bank of the canal within hearing distance all the way to Albany, which were discharged in turn, and thus the departure of the *Seneca Chief* from Buffalo was announced at Albany in one hour and forty minutes, then the fastest dispatch time on record.

The Black Rock dignitaries, not then reconstructed from their civil war with Buffalonians, declined to join Buffalo in celebrating , but chartered the new boat *Niagara*, built by the late Josiah Beardsley to run as a packet to and from Lockport, which they had painted and decorated profusely, carrying a large, live eagle perched aloft on a standard, for their passage down the canal. Intending to lead the *Seneca Chief* through the state, they started from Black Rock two hours in advance of that boat's scheduled time from Buffalo, but such design was frustrated by an order of Governor Clinton that no boat be passed through the locks eastward in advance of the *Seneca Chief*. The Black Rock party consisted of General Porter, Sheldon Thompson, Lester Brace, and a Mr. Mason. Eventually all became reconciled and were potent factors in promoting the interests of Buffalo, Mr. Thompson becoming mayor of the city in 1840, and Mr. Brace for two terms was sheriff of the county.

The visit to Buffalo of General Lafayette the same year was an event tending to arouse latent patriotic enthusiasm. American gratitude to the liberty-promoting foreigner was boundless, and his reception at Buffalo was most enthusiastic. The communities of Western New York gathered in mass to greet him. On a platform, erected at the corner of Court and Main streets, he was introduced to the mass of people by General Porter, and the address of welcome there made to him by Oliver Forward was considered the most dignified and eloquent presented to the General while in the country. Red Jacket, also, improved his opportunity to have a "big talk." When the ceremony was ended, the General was escorted by the military and citizens to the residence of General Porter, at Black Rock, where he was entertained for a day, and then, in like manner, was escorted to the Falls.

By far the most sensational event of the year was the hanging of the three Thayers in open view on Niagara Square. Sufficiently sensational to stir up a much larger community—sufficient to cause the invasion of the town by full twenty thousand visitors, a number sufficient to overwhelm a struggling village of two thousand inhabitants.

Lafayette Park, now classic ground, was, in village times, an open space, with here and there a tree of indigenous growth. On the Main street edge, fronting the site of the monument, a spring of water bubbled out of the earth and ran a rivulet across the street and down Court street, finally mingling with a larger stream crossing Niagara at Mohawk street. At the spring the side-path was continued over a wide oaken plank spanning the outlet. Here Farmer's Brother, Red Jacket and other lords of the soil were wont to quench their thirst, drinking from a tin cup taken from the top of a buttonwood stump near by; here the village boys played two-old-cat, tag and leap-frog, and on the Fourth of July exploded firecrackers and gorged themselves with gingerbread and small-beer; here village orators waxed eloquent advocating the construction of the Erie Canal, and a harbor for Buffalo; here General McComb, when head of the army, patriotically addressed the people, and Henry Clay, Daniel Webster and the patriot Kossuth orated in like manner. The beautiful Soldiers' Monument stands on the direct line of march of the three Thayers down Court street to their execution on Niagara square; and six years later, Holt, the wife-killer, marched in procession to his open-air exhibition.

In 1932 Buffalo will celebrate its centennial—just one hundred years a city. From the base of the monument the orator of the day will glorify the deeds of the heroes it commemorates and boast of the progress of Buffalo, quoting from the address of Mayor Grover Cleveland delivered from the same place fifty years before.

The little park came nigh unto being the scene of a hand-to-hand conflict between village neighbors on election day in 1828. The voting place was at the corner of Clinton and Washington streets. On the eve of the election the partisans of General Jackson erected a hickory flag-staff on the opposite corner and from its top they proposed to fly a flag on the day of the election bearing a likeness of their candidate for President. The Adams men objected to the flaunting of the, to them, offensive emblem so near to the polls, and resolutely declared that if the flag was raised they would pull it down, forcibly if they must. The Jacksonians asserted their right to fly the flag and their determination to raise it and to defend it when raised. Such was the situation on the eve of the election.

On Buffalo Plains were resident a band of stalwart men noted for their prowess and of their proneness to assert it when occasion offered. Of these were included Elijah and William Holt, John and Josiah Hosford, Rowland and Daniel Cotton, John and Jacob Scott, Luman Smith and Nelson Adams, a Spartan band of Jacksonians, loaded to the muzzle with campaign enthusiasm.

To the "Plains Rangers," as they were called, the village partisans of "Old Hickory" applied for aid to defend their flag. On the morning of the election the flag was hoisted to the pole-top. Then the Adams men gathered in numbers at the Park House, corner of Main and Clinton streets, where an assaulting force was organized, who proceeded in a body to demand the lowering of the flag. When they approached the flag-staff and discovered the Plains contingent among those whom they were to encounter, a halt was called, a consultation, and then a dispersion of the attacking force. No demand was made and the flag waved, and General Jackson was elected President without bloodshed in Buffalo. Thus was exemplified the maxim: To promote peace prepare for war—and the folly of partisan rancor.

Preserved in frame by the Historical Society is an old ball ticket of the village era, unique in print, and rural in that the assemblage is requested to meet at two o'clock P. M. Evidently the small hours of the morning were devoted to rest and sleep by the dancers of the period. However, they danced with both feet while the fiddler voiced in a manner thus:

>Right hand across, left hand back,
>Keep your steps in time.
>Take hold of your partner's hand
>And balance in a line.

CHAPTER VI.

During the village era an adjacent community to Buffalo villagers were the settlers of Buffalo Plains, with whom they lived in the same township, met at the polls, socially and at church, virtually one community. The Plains were originally settled by a colony of farmers from the lake region of Central New York. First to come on a tour of inspection was Samuel Atkins, in 1806, from Cayuga, on horseback, traversing Indian trails through a dense forest to Buffalo—not to speculate in village lots, but to purchase farm lands for himself and others who desired to settle near unto the site of the great city that was to arise at the foot of Lake Erie.

Mr. Atkins remained at Buffalo through the summer, returning to Cayuga in the fall of that year. Before his return he engaged for himself and others tracts of land lying on the "Main Road" from four to six miles from the hamlet at the foot of the lake, in a northeast direction; selecting for himself about three hundred acres on the east side and midway of the tract, on which, while at Buffalo in 1806, he erected a house of logs wherein to place his family the following year.

In the spring of 1807, there left Cayuga with their families, Samuel Atkins, Ephraim Brown, Ezekiel Smith, Rowland Cotton, Roswell Hosford, William and Elijah Holt, Caleb and Joseph Fairchild; all on horseback, with such household effects as could be so transported. The year following they were joined by the families of Zachary Griffin and Dr. Daniel Chapin. All of these took up lands and formed the old community of farmers who were the original settlers of Buffalo Plains. Nearly all were soldiers of the Revolution and drew pensions from the Government, and had grown-up sons and daughters skilled in husbandry. Mr. Atkins' family consisted of five sons and two daughters; three of the sons and both daughters were approaching maturity—a formidable force to make a new home in a new country. With the exception of Mr. Cotton and the Holts, the heads of all these families occupied their new-made homes during the remainder of their lives. In 1826 Mr. Cotton sold his farm to Washington A. Russell and settled in the town of Lancaster; and subsequently the Holts sold theirs to Elisha Ensign and removed to Ohio.

The frontage of the Griffin farm is now divided by the Belt Line railroad as it approaches Main street from the south. The Chapin farm now comprises beautiful Willow Lawn, the home of Mrs. Elam R. Jewett, and the southerly half of Park Meadow, including the magnificent groves, lawns and terraces fringing the north bank of Park Lake. The frontage of the Cotton farm continues in occupation by the son and daughters of Mr. Russell, while the remainder comprises the site of modern dwellings on Parkside, together with the northerly half of Park Meadow and picturesque Park Forest. The Holt and Smith farms are now the place of extensive stone quarries and waterlime works; and the Brown farm, lying opposite the County Almshouse, is mostly an unoccupied waste; and so is the Fairchild property, situated on the west side of the road just north of the Lackawanna Railroad crossing.

The old domain of Samuel Atkins is now a desolate and neglected ruin. Where once were fields of golden grain, orchards and gardens of luxuriant production, is now covered with a riotous growth of weed, brier and thistle. The engines of two railroads toot and hoot over the waste, consonant with its presentment, an owl's abiding-place.

For several years past this realty has been the subject of continued and costly litigation. When a young man, it was to the writer a barren inheritance, and ever since a plague spot in memory.

On this property, in 1807, Mr. Atkins erected a majestic structure of logs, consisting of three separate buildings, made so by two dividing passages through the lower story, while the upper story and roof remained intact. The building entire was eighteen by eighty feet on the ground, with sides thirteen feet high—quite an imposing frontier establishment. Here Mr. Atkins kept a tavern, a house of

HOUSE OF ANNA ATKINS.

entertainment for travelers and pilgrims journeying to the new West. Many veterans of the war of the Revolution had settled on the Niagara frontier, and the old log tavern was their headquarters—was where they held their camp-fires and fought their battles anew. To a man they sustained the policy of President Madison to maintain the majesty of the starry flag on the high seas. In possession of the writer is a printed poster, dated April 16, 1811, calling a meeting for such purpose at the old tavern. The time-bleached paper and quaint type characterizes it a veritable spirit of liberty and independence.

The old tavern was the refuge of many fleeing families from torch and tomahawk on that fatal day and night of 1813, from burning Buffalo. The house survived until 1823, when it was replaced by the large frame structure long known as the "Old Homestead."

The house erected by Mr. Atkins in 1806 was subsequently the district school-house, in which, during the decade of the thirties, the writer attended school. His education was there hastened to completion by the pungent rawhide, wielded by the strong arms of sundry esteemed pedagogues, the most severe of whom posed as an orthodox Christian. But he died one day, and the conviction that he was thereafter kept warm amidst the glare of the Calvinistic process, gave consolation to his victims. Woodward! thou are not lost to memory dear—thy fame is here perpetuated. The site of the old school-house is now buried beneath the embankment of the D., L. & W. Railroad at its Main street crossing.

Of the original settlers of Buffalo Plains, first and second generations alike have vanished—

> "Gone like tenants who quit without warning,
> Down the back entry of time."

With two exceptions all the old buildings erected by the pioneers of Buffalo Plains have disappeared. The residence of Zachary Griffin, erected in 1809, and a house erected in 1817 by Anna Atkins, widow of Samuel, are still in evidence just east of the Belt Line crossing. Ephraim Brown was the eldest of these old settlers, reaching the age of eighty years at his death sixty years ago. The old war-worn veteran with cane in hand would limp among the school children, who would flock around to hear him recite the story of his battles, and to hear him chant the army rhymes of the good old Colony times. The old man was stalwart of frame, but quite lame, the effect of a musket ball penetrating his knee at the battle of Trenton. With children grouped around him "Old Mr. Brown" would sing thus:

> A haughty ship o'er the ocean came,
> All loaded deep with fire and flame,
> And other things I need not name,
> To have a "dash at Stonington."
>
> The old razee, with hot ball,
> Did make a farmer's barrack fall,
> And a codfish fleet did sadly maul,
> About one mile from Stonington.
>
> Now some assert on certain grounds,
> Beside the damage and the wounds,
> It cost King George ten thousand pounds
> To have a "dash at Stonington."

Buffalo Plains has a war record. In the fall of 1812 the Army of the Frontier went into winter quarters on Flint Hill. The camp extended on Main street from the present Humboldt parkway northerly to the lands of Dr. Daniel Chapin, now the Jewett property, and westerly to the head of Park Lake, on lands belonging to Erastus Granger, then

ZACHARY GRIFFIN HOMESTEAD.

Collector of Customs and Postmaster of Buffalo. On the Main street front of this old camp-ground stand several venerable oaks, relicts of the old camp. The one directly opposite the Deaf and Dumb Asylum is distinguished as the one under which a row of soldiers kneeled when shot for desertion in the spring of 1813. The venerable oaks are still vigorous, but their lives are in danger. The land boomer and builder covet the space they occupy and they may soon disappear from view. Boomer, spare those trees, let the old oaks stand!

CHAPTER VII.

At the advent of the steamboat in 1818, Lake Erie was navigated by a fleet of small sail craft, fully adequate for the commerce then existing between points on the lake. An early enrollment reads:

Sch. *Experiment*, 30 tons. Samuel Wilkeson and James Hale, owners. Samuel Wilkeson, master.

Captain Wilkeson lost his nautical title when Judge on the bench, and Mayor of Buffalo. A clearance dated November, 1819, reads:

Cleared, Sch. *Nautilus*, 26 tons, Atkins, master, for Cleveland and Sandusky, with passengers and household goods.

Eager to emigrate to the new West in 1819, families would pack themselves with their goods on board a diminutive sail craft, and brave the perils of turbulent Lake Erie in the tempestuous month of November. Yet there are people who discount the valor of our forefathers.

Guy J. Atkins, master of the *Nautilus,* was a valiant defender of Buffalo and the frontier during the war of 1812, an associate of Dr. Cyrenius Chapin in his several raids for reprisals during the conflict.

The sailing fleet tributary to Buffalo when assuming the dignity of a city, comprised about fifty small schooners and sloops, three or four of which had smelled powder in the battle of Lake Erie. Notably among them was the schooner *Queen Charlotte,* a 200-ton vessel. Having been naturalized amid the roar of artillery, she sailed the lake a merchantman several years thereafter. Prior to 1836 she was under the command of Capt. Lester H. Cotton, a life resident of Buffalo—one of the "old folks."

The first sail-vessel to clear from Buffalo, bound for Chicago, was the brig *Illinois* Capt. James Shook, in 1834. An historic vessel was the schooner *John Kinsie,* she bringing the first cargo of wheat to Buffalo out of Lake Michigan, 3,000 bushels from Grand River. Regular shipments of grain from Lake Michigan commenced in 1840. That year Chicago shipped 10,000 bushels of wheat to Buffalo. In 1836 the lakes were sailed by two full-rigged ships, the *Julia Palmer,* Capt. Robt. Wagstaff, and the *Milwaukie,* Capt. William Dickson. Captains Wagstaff and Dickson were old Neptunes of the lakes, and long residents of Buffalo. The old homestead of Captain Dickson is still in existence on Barker street, but not as secluded as when occupied by him fifty years ago.

Notably among the vessels that were in commission on the lakes in 1840, were three brigs, the *Illinois,* Capt. James Shook, *North Carolina* Capt. Gus. McKinstry, and *Indiana,* Capt. Aaron Root. Asaph S. Bemis was then mate of the *Indiana.* These men were web-footed, and sailed the Great Lakes with audacity and impunity. Many acquaintances of A. S. Bemis in his later life were not aware of the fact that he was an experienced navigator. He had many

The Steamer Buffalo—1838.

commands, his last being the steamboat *Star* in 1841-42. Private interests caused his retirement from a profession he loved and honored.

The sailing fleet of 1835-36 included the following vessels and masters:

BRIGS.	CAPTAINS.
Illinois,	Robert Wagstaff.
Indiana,	Augustus McKinstry.
North Carolina,	Aaron Root.

SCHOONERS.	CAPTAINS.
Nucleus,	Thomas P. Folger.
President,	Benjamin Sweet.
Globe,	Zeph Perkins.
Hercules,	Benjamin Boomer.
Michigan,	William Dickson.
Telegraph,	Peter Smith.
Bolivar,	C. H. Ludlow.
Queen Charlotte,	L. H. Cotton.
Buffalo,	Robert Hart.
Henry Norton,	Jerry Oliver.
Warren,	George Montieth.
Nancy Dousman,	James Shook.
Marie Antoinette,	Edward Macy.
Panama,	Richard Meeks.
Thomas Hart,	Thomas Melville.
Daniel Webster,	J. D. Moon.
John Grant,	John Nelson.
Florida,	N. K. Randall.
Young Amaranth,	J. W. Ransom.
Alabama,	Abner Smith.
Commerce,	Reuben Smith.
Hiram,	Ezra Rathbun.
John Adams,	J. A. Barker.
Cincinnati,	William Dorrit.
Post Boy,	Morgan Edgecomb.
John Richards,	R. Ferguson.
L. Jenkins,	Daniel Fuller.

SCHOONERS.	CAPTAINS.
Ware,	John Garnsey.
Comet,	Seth Green.
Benjamin Rusk,	Augustus Todd.
Marshal Ney,	Lyman Harvey.
La Porte,	Benjamin Owen.
Constitution,	A. H. Squier.
Columbus,	David Clark.
Dewitt Clinton,	William Christian.
Agnes Barton,	J. G. Ludlow.
Ben Franklin,	Samuel Blackley.
United States,	Edward Burke.
Eclipse,	John Berg.
Wyandotte,	B. Black.
Alert,	Walter Atwell.
Farmer,	Hugh Soper.
Navigator,	James Thorpe.
Enterprise,	W. S. Thorpe.
John C. Spencer,	Stephen Walker,
Lewis Goler,	John Warren.
Thomas Hart,	David White.
Col. Crockett,	John Whitney.
Philipps,	Charles Howe.
New Connecticut,	William Kennedy.
Duke of Wellington,	John Medler.

After the loss of the original boat, and during the village era, eleven steamboats were constructed for the navigation of the lake, ten of which were in commission when the city was inaugurated. Appended are their names, and the names of their commanders:

STEAMBOATS.	CAPTAINS.
Superior,	William T. Pease.
Niagara, No. 1,	Charles C. Stanard.
Henry Clay,	Walter Norton.
Sheldon Thompson,	Augustus Walker.
William Penn,	David Wight.
William Peacock,	Thomas Wilkins.
Pioneer,	Charles Burnett.
Ohio,	Morris Tyler.
Enterprise,	George Niles.
Caroline,	James Pettey.

The *Peacock* made tri-weekly trips to Conneaut, calling at Erie, Dunkirk and Barcelona. The *Caroline* ran Niagara River to Chippewa and Schlosser dock. The remainder ran to Sandusky and Detroit. At first some one of the boats would extend one trip to Mackinaw and Green Bay each season. In 1834 the *Pioneer* was wrecked on Lake Michigan when on such a trip. The *Michigan* came out during the summer of 1832, commanded by Capt. Chesley Blake. Her first service was a trip to Green Bay, conveying General Scott, with a body of troops, for service in the Black Hawk War. During the passage cholera broke out on board, causing many deaths, principally among the troops.

At this period there were four Canadian steamboats in commission, mostly confined to home waters, one of which, the *Thames*, commanded by Captain Van Allen, carried on trade with Buffalo. Mr. Van Allen, subsequently, was proprietor of the Clarendon Hotel in Buffalo. Excepting the *William Penn*, owned by Rufus Reed, of Erie, all the American fleet were controlled at Buffalo, and their crews resided there. Such was the steam fleet of Lake Erie sixty-six years ago. Their combined tonnage was less than 2,000 tons. Recently a lake steamer was launched from a

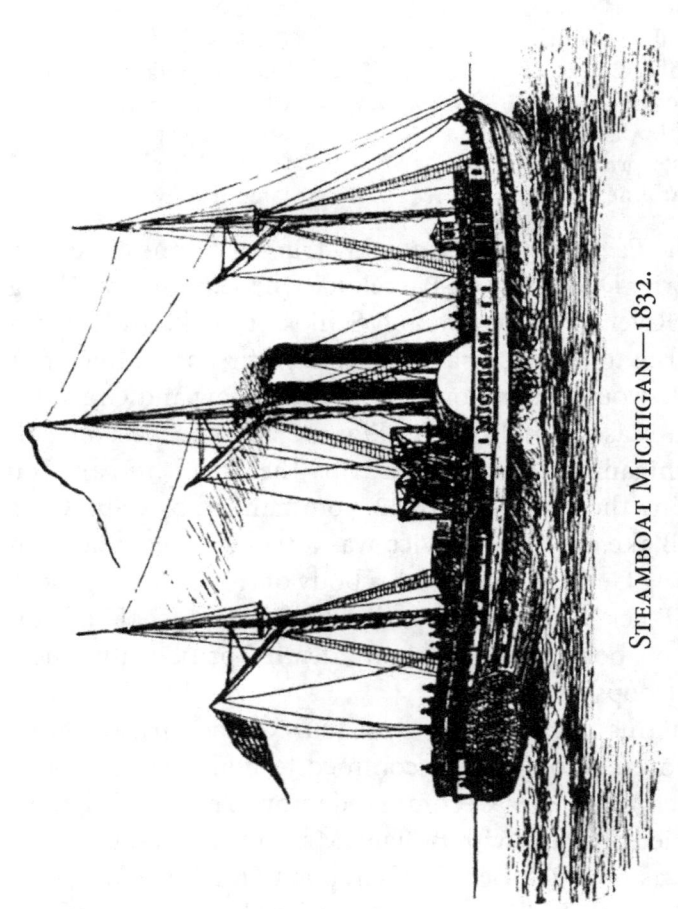

STEAMBOAT MICHIGAN—1832.

Buffalo ship-yard, not of the larger class, yet double the tonnage of the ten pioneer boats combined.

The first steamboat to run the Niagara in regular route, was the *Caroline* brought from Albany through the canal for the purpose, by shipping her guards. In 1834 the *Victory*, eighty-seven tons, was built for the river route. She was commanded by Capt. John Hebard. In 1840 Capt. C. L. Gager built the *Red Jacket* for the route, but she was soon taken to the St. Clair River. Then on the river appeared in turn the *Sun*, *Star* and *Waterloo*, and finally the *Emerald*, a Canadian vessel, which plied the river for a number of years. After the *Emerald* came the *Arrow*, a good boat, and after her the *Clifton*, the best of all. But the railroad to the Falls forced them to seek traffic on the upper rivers.

Apparently the founding of a city on the shore of Lake Erie in 1832, was an incentive to ship-building, as the next year twelve new steamboats were added to the fleet. Seven others came in 1834, and a like number in 1835. With one exception the new boats were a slight improvement upon the old fleet. The exception was the *Washington*, built in 1833, the largest and best found boat so far appearing on the lake. But her career was limited to three trips. Encountering a violent tempest on her third passage up the lake, she was wrecked on Long Point, a total loss. Then another steamboat appeared named the *Washington*, which was soon after burned on the lake, and since then the name *Washington*, for a lake vessel, has been neglected by ship-owners. Later there was a lake boat named *Lady Washington*, which escaped serious disaster.

In Black Rock harbor, a short distance above the ship-lock, when the water is clear, may be seen on the bottom the wrecks of the early steamboats *Henry Clay*, *North America* and *Daniel Webster*, there moored as cast-aways,

THE THOMAS JEFFERSON—1834.

in 1842, to relieve crowded Buffalo Creek. These boats were not over-aged when retired, but their primitive construction rendered them useless to compete with the more modern boats then in commission.

The following named steamboats were navigating the lakes in 1835-36:

STEAMBOATS.	CAPTAINS.
Michigan	Chesley Blake.
Thomas Jefferson,	Thomas Wilkins.
Sandusky,	T. J. Titus.
Daniel Webster,	Morris Tyler.
General Porter,	Walter Norton.
United States,	A. E. Hart.
Charles Townsend,	Simeon Fox.
Pennsylvania,	Levi Allen.

STEAMBOATS.	CAPTAINS.
Monroe,	Harry Whittaker.
Commodore Perry,	David Wilkinson.
Oliver Newberry,	A. Edwards.
William Penn,	David Wright.
William Peacock,	E. W. Pratt.
North America.	Gilman Appleby.
Ohio,	Charles Burnett.
Detroit,	R. Gillett.
Delaware,	Captain Cobb.
Victory,	John Hebard.
Caroline,	James Pettey.
Governor Marcy,	Samuel Chase.
Oswego,	James Homaus.

As a class the lake navigators of the period were men of striking individuality. Dobbins, Pease, Stanard, Norton, Allen, Blake, Wilkeson, Burnett, Chamberlain, Lundy, Cotton, Wilkins, Wilkinson, Titus, Shainholdts, Walker, Ludlow, Goldsmith, Brundage, Fox, Folger, Pratt, Hart, Floyd, Squier, Randall, Whittaker, Wagstaff, Dickson, Caverly, Hinton, Wilson, Shook, Hazard, Nickerson, Stewart, Sweet, Perkins, Pheatt, Traverse, Bemis, Peter Smith, McBride, Averill, Gager, Appleby, Webster, Dorr, Wheeler, Atwood, Vary, Stone, Snow, Arthur, Watts, Hathaway, Huff, Howland, and others of like caliber, were a class who, seemingly, arose for the requirements of the time; bold and intrepid navigators, marking their courses without artificial aid—no charts, no buoys nor harbors of refuge, a paucity of lights, no guides other than the compass, the eye, the watch and the lead, the lakes not being navigated at that time by governmental appliances.

During this era of flush steam-boating there was a world of emigration to the West—to Michigan, Wisconsin Indiana and Illinois, mostly from the farming communities of the Eastern States and the State of New York. The wharves at Buffalo, from the opening to the close of navigation, were crowded with these people, packing their household goods, farm implements, farm animals and themselves on board steamboats, bound for new homes in the productive West. Such congregations of people caused Buffalo to be the Mecca for hordes of snide operators, fakirs, nostrum venders, the pestiferous watch-stuffer, and other birds of prey, who flocked there to impose on the simplicity of the credulous emigrants. Notwithstanding that steamboat officers and others were diligent in warning unsuspecting strangers to beware of these inhuman sharks, they found victims in abundance.

Then the era of illustrious steam-boating on Lake Erie was at its zenith. A fleet of magnificent passenger boats, luxurious in appointments, officered by skilled navigators, picturesque in ruffled linen and affability, no dearth of patronage, a world of travel, fair women and brave men, bands of music galore—hurrah, boys! from the commencement to the close of each season, until that autocrat of the rail—the locomotive—relegated the passenger steamer to inactivity during the decade of the fifties.

The steamboat officers were active in prosecuting the boom, all partaking of the spirit of the times. Among those resident at Buffalo were the following captains:

L. H. Cotton,	Henry Randall,	C. M. Averill,
Levi Allen,	Harry Whittaker,	George Willoughby,
T. J. Titus,	Gilman Appleby,	C. E. Roby.
C. H. Ludlow,	Morris Hazard,	Charles Brundage,
John Hebard,	Luther Chamberlain,	Ira Davis,
W. T. Pease,	C. C. Stanard,	H. Van Allen,
A. S. Bemis,	Simeon Fox,	F. N. Jones,
John Shook,	A. H. Squier,	A. D. Perkins,
Augustus Walker,	Heber Squier,	F. S. Wheeler,

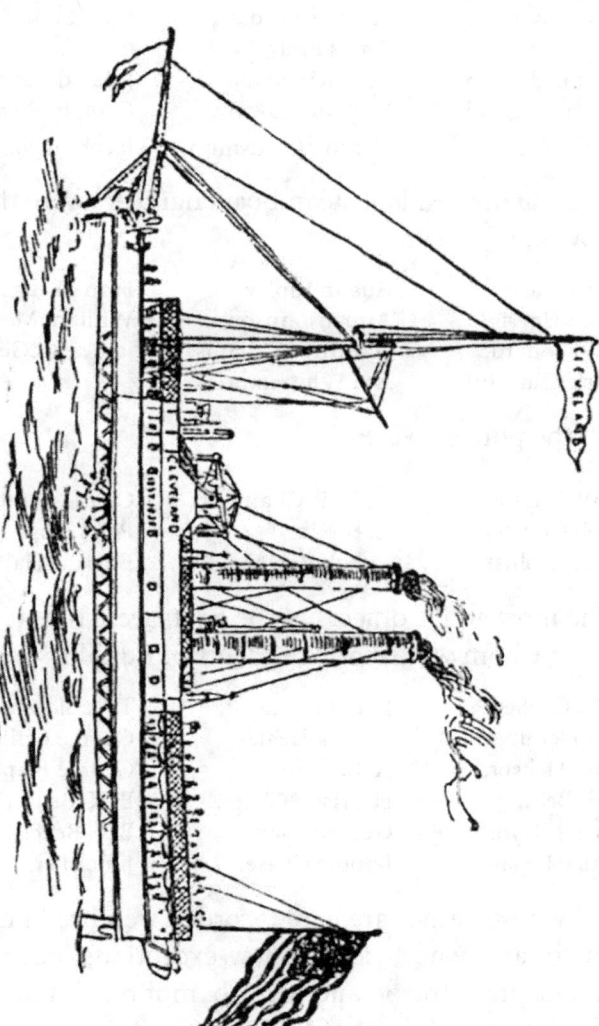

The Old Cleveland—1838.

Benjamin Stanard,	James Shook,	William Davenport,
James N. Lundy,	Samuel Vary,	F. S. Miller,
George W. Floyd,	Peter Shainholdts,	Captain Robertson,
Charles Burnett,	Thomas P. Folger,	W. P. Stone,
A. E. Hart,	Amos Pratt,	C. L. Gager,
Archibald Allen,	A. T. Kingman,	J. L. Edmunds,
Robert Wagstaff,	William Caverly,	Captain Pierce,
Walter Norton,	Clinton Goldsmith,	Jacob Imson.

Among the resident steamboat engineers were the following:

Albert Harris,	Austin Ripley,	Frank Peugeot,
Alfred Harris,	Almar Johnson,	William McGee,
John Leonard,	Gardner Williams,	James McGee.
Charles Radcliff,	Asa Whittemore,	

Of the pursers were:

M. W. Dayton,	O. H. P. Champlin,	Charles Addington,
Ralph Courter,	C. B. Rice,	Peter Hoyt,
John J. Hollister,	Joseph Barton,	Edward Hallenbeck.

The most active officers of the boats were the stewards, among whom were many residents of Buffalo:

W. G. Corbett,	James Delano,	T. T. Bloomer,
John Fleming,	Patrick Healey,	George Gillispie,
Frank Jackson,	A. B. Catlin,	George Blanchard,
Jacob Bellinger,	Harrison Chase,	E. K. Bruce,
Charles Baylis,	George Ayers,	B. F. Bruce,
Bartley Logan,	Jerome Chase,	J. Bunker.

All whose names are here recorded were well known in Buffalo, and who, with but few exceptions, have passed away. Captain Imson and Mr. Champlin still remain, old and venerated citizens of Buffalo.

At this period winter was the dull season in Buffalo. With the close of navigation, travel other than by stage lines was suspended. With resident lake navigators it was a season of social enjoyment, and with their round of pleasures, sleighing and dancing, they made things lively. Their motto was "Melancholy must go." With them it was:

> "To some ball, to some play,
> With some party every day,
> Drinking wine with
> Some gentlemen or other."

Of this festive squadron Capt. Fred Wheeler was the admiral. His associates were kept on the alert lest they became victims of his jokes and surprises.

On the southeast corner of Main and Swan streets was Deacon Stocking's hat and fur store. Next below was the ribbon and bonnet store of John F. Williams, usually called "Bonnet Williams," and by Captain Wheeler, "The He Milliner"—a man noted for his quiet humor, and for his close friendship with Capt. Fred Wheeler.

It was a sunny morning in the month of April, when Captain Wheeler, awaiting the opening of navigation, came strolling up the street. Williams was having his store cellar renovated. The refuse was thrown up on the sidewalk. Capt. Wheeler protested to having the walk so obstructed. Williams replied that the wheelbarrow and shovel there standing was awaiting a man out of a job, and advised the Captain of his opportunity to work and earn something, offering him ten cents for each load of dirt that he would wheel and dump in the rear. This proposition Captain Wheeler accepted, and at once plied the shovel in loading the barrow. When returning from the dump, he took fright at a buffalo-skin which Deacon Stocking was displaying on his awning frame and ran away with the wheel-barrow. Starting rapidly, he carromed on a gaily-dressed dummy standing at the front of Williams's store, capsizing and decapitating the fair one. Wildly on he ran, down the street, into the Terrace, where, in collision with the Liberty Pole, the wheelbarrow was shattered into many parts and the runaway captured by Asa D. Wood and A. J. Tiffany, who led him into the Mansion House, where in time he became quieted. No lives lost; damage, about twenty dollars.

Once upon a time a dance-house flourished on the Lower Terrace, facing the canal. The upper story of the structure was even with the ground at its rear, where there was a lone window. Capt. Fred Wheeler, with companions, were passing by one evening, when they observed through the rear window a party of dancers skipping the light fantastic in high glee. On the ground near by lay an unmounted grindstone, some four feet in diameter. The grindstone was raised and taken to the bank in the rear of the dance-house, to which the down grade was about forty degrees. When the stone was started it rolled accurately, passing through the window and speeding on through the maze of dancers and through the front of the building into the canal, where, perhaps, it remains imbedded in the mud bottom. The consternation of the dancers at the sudden invasion of the grindstone may be imagined. A description would be difficult to write and do justice to the subject. I have ever more than suspected that my old friend and ex-County Treasurer, Charles R. Durkee, was an actor in that comedy.

My first steamboat ride was in the summer of 1837. In company with my mother and young sister, we went to the foot of Main street and boarded the steamboat *William Penn* bound for Dunkirk, to visit relatives. Being a youth of eleven years I was in affluence in having in my pocket a silver half-dollar, pocket money for the journey. To those who first go to sea in ships, seasickness is a dreaded anticipation. Prior to the departure of the boat there appeared to the passengers a long-haired, lop-eared, lantern-jawed, lank and limp specimen of humanity, soliciting them to purchase his panacea for seasickness—vials filled with a pink-colored solution of aqua, cinnamon essence and rose-water.

THE WILLIAM PENN—1826.

Through his superlative assurance, aided by simplicity, he caught me. O, he "played it that day upon me in a way I despise"—relieved me of one-half of my capital at the outset of my journey. The picturesque perpetrator of the commodity, designed to cure all diseases of mind, body and estate, could not have perfected it, for the boat had not proceeded more than a mile seaward from the lighthouse, before the dreaded malady had marked me for its own.

The appropriation of a locomotive, and run off successfully, is an event of recent date, but the theft of a steamboat, successfully consummated, was an enterprise of a former era. During the latter thirties was built the steamboat *Milwaukie* a vessel designed more for speed than a bearer of burdens. In 1841 she was owned jointly by parties of Buffalo and Milwaukee, between whom arose a legal controversy relative to their several interests in the

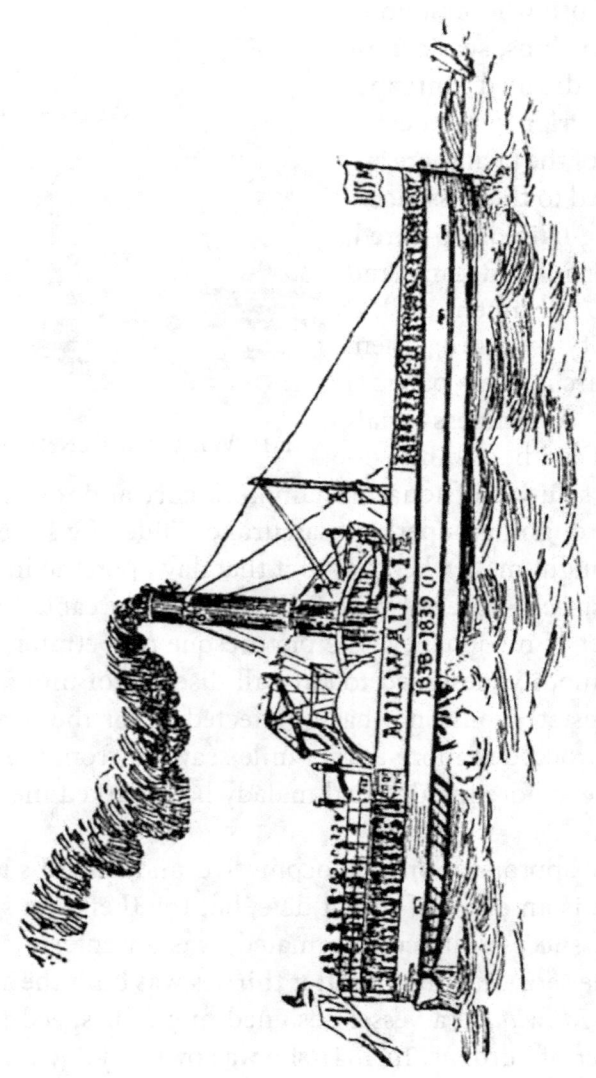

The Famous Milwaukie—1838.

steamboat. When the steamer was at the port of Buffalo she was laid up in ordinary in charge of a shipkeeper, on the principle that possession was points in the game. In the meantime the Milwaukee owners were reticent while hatching a scheme to obtain possession of the property in dispute by strategy. To manage the enterprise they employed Capt. L. H. Cotton, who organized a trusty crew and rendezvoused at Buffalo. On an August night of 1841, the boat was boarded, the shipkeeper seized, gagged and confined, steam raised, the moorings cast off, when the boat cautiously passed out onto the lake, and away she went, too speedy to be overtaken by any craft on the lakes. Buffalo owners were compelled to accept the situation, there being no means to head off the fugitive, telegraph poles not then standing in line over the country. The following day Buffalo newspapers announced thus:

> LOST, STRAYED OR STOLEN—The low-pressure steamboat *Milwaukie* was last seen before day-break this morning rounding the lighthouse and skipping over the waters of Lake Erie. A liberal reward awaits whoever effects her arrest before reaching Lake Michigan.

Their first landing was at Silver Creek pier, where they liberated their prisoner, and helped themselves to a few cords of wood there convenient, and then made a straight wake to Put-in-Bay Island, where more fuel was obtained. They then rapidly passed through the rivers to Lake Huron and on to Milwaukee, where she was run hard aground inside the mouth of the river, there to remain until sold to Oliver Newberry, of Detroit, who placed her engine and boilers in his new steamboat *Nile*.

On May 12, 1844, the steamboat *Rochester* left the foot of Main street, Buffalo, bound for Chicago, officered as follows: Thomas P. Folger, master; Harry Weishuen, mate; William McGee, engineer; O. H. P. Champlin, clerk; Bartley Logan, steward.

During his mechanical work engineer McGee had constructed a small steam-whistle, patterned from plans published in the *Scientific American* which he attached to the boiler of the *Rochester* more for its novelty than for its utility. Before the boat left the wharf the whistle was sounded, the first to give voice in the region of the Great Lakes. Prior to the whistle, loud-sounding bells were hung above decks on all lake vessels, which supplied the needs of the present steam-whistle.

During the winter preceding, Capt. C. L. Gager had made a propeller out of the old steamboat *General Porter*. Between Gager and McGee an old feud existed. A few miles below Mackinaw the *Rochester* overhauled the *Porter* and when passing her McGee blew his whistle persistently and defiantly. The steamboat landed at Mackinaw, as also did the propeller. Being unaware that McGee was engineer of the *Rochester*, Gager appeared at the steamboat dock and loudly demanded to be shown the man who "squawked that thing at him." McGee was prompt in leaping on the wharf and shouting, "Take a look at me!" Then came a resolute intervention of mutual friends preventing war between two stalwart men. And thus was demonstrated the utility of the steam-whistle and its inauguration on the Great Lakes without bloodshed.

In general, early lake steamboats were officered by sailors who gained their experience on the fleet of sailing vessels navigating Lake Erie prior to the advent of the steamboat. A notable exception occurred at the outset, when Captain Fish was imported from the North River to command the *Walk-in-the-Water*. When navigating Lake

Erie, Captain Fish encountered, to him, a novel experience. During a storm on the lake, Captain Fish became seasick—utterly demoralized—when passengers and crew insisted that mate Davis should assume command of the vessel. This being done, the steamboat was safely navigated through the storm; and for the remainder of the season it was Captain Davis, while Captain Fish returned to swim in the more placid waters surrounding Manhattan Island. Thereafter, as a rule, lake steamboats were commanded by lake sailors.

Later, however, a more flagrant case occurred which aroused the indignation of lake shipmasters. About 1846, Capt. Henry Randall sold the steamboat *Wisconsin* to William Chard, a gentleman largely engaged in canal transportation. Mr. Chard was an expert in canal navigation, but in no sense a lake navigator. Mr. Chard, firstly, changed the orthography of the name of the boat to *Wiskonsan* and then, as a business proposition, assumed the command, and then the trouble commenced. A "canaler" master of a lake steamboat, was an absurdity intolerable, and war was declared against Mr. Chard and his steamboat *Wiskonsan*. An emblematic war—a war of ridicule was diligently waged. In addition to the blowing of horns and shouting "low bridge," canal harness and whiffletrees were run aloft on other boats when meeting the *Wiskonsan*. Steamboat agents were diligent in advising travelers that the master of the *Wiskonsan* was a landsman, a factor most potent in diverting patronage, and Mr. Chard concluded that business demanded a lake navigator for the master of his steamboat, and the demand being supplied, hostilities ended and peace was restored. Mr. Chard was energetic in business and social in intercourse with all whom he met, and subsequently was popular in navigation circles.

In 1852 the General Government assumed jurisdiction of the Great Lakes, when knowledge and experience became indispensable for a commission to command a lake vessel.

The serious disasters occurring during the era of side-wheel steam-boating, in the main consisted of the burning of the *Washington*, *Erie* and *G. P. Griffith* on Lake Erie and the *Niagara* and *Sea Bird* on Lake Michigan; the sinking by collision of the *Atlantic* and *Chesapeake* on Lake Erie, and the *Lady Elgin* on Lake Michigan; the foundering of the *Sunbeam* on Lake Superior, and the *Keystone State* on Lake Huron. All of these casualties were attended with the loss of human life in a degree horrifying, unless that of the *Chesapeake* be the exception.

The *Washington* in 1838, and the *Erie* in 1841, were burned when on an upward passage, both at the same point on the lake, off Silver Creek, thirty-five miles out of Buffalo. The steamboat *Griffith* was burned off Fairport, on an upward trip, her passengers and crew being driven overboard by the rapid spreading of the flames. Captain Roby and wife, clasped in each other's arms, thus met their death. In 1860 the steamboat *Lady Elgin* in command of Capt. John Wilson, was running between the ports of Lake Michigan and Lake Superior. At Milwaukee she gave an evening excursion to the firemen of that city. The boat was crowded with men, women and children. The night was dark and misty, and the water was rough; without warning a sailing vessel crashed into the steamer, then glanced off and was seen no more, while the boat, loaded with humanity, sank beneath the waters. When the boat sunk the hurricane deck floated in two sections, upon which officers of the sunken steamer placed many passengers. The shore was distant a mile or more, with the wind blowing on, towards which the rafts drifted. The one carrying Captain Wilson reached the shore intact, but the other broke up in the breakers. To assist the women and children struggling in the angry surf, Captain Wilson rushed in, but the frantic sufferers seized hold of him in numbers, and he was drowned with them. Thus heroically perished Captain Jack Wilson, a brave and popular lake sailor. Three days later the steamboat *North Star,* Capt. Ben Sweet, arrived at the Soo, bringing the sad news of the loss of the *Lady Elgin*. The veteran Captain Lundy was standing on the wharf. Captain Sweet locked arms with him, and the two elderly men walked slowly in the direction of the hotel, where boarded the wife of Capt. Jack Wilson. Arm in arm they ascended the hotel stairs. At the top Captain Lundy halted, while Captain Sweet proceeded to the door of Mrs. Wilson's apartment. The old sailor raised his arm to knock at the door, hesitated, and then withdrew, and said, "Lundy, I can't!" Then the other old sailor essayed to perform the mournful errand, but also returned and said, "Sweet, I can't!" Then the veterans of many battles with the elements slowly descended the stairs, while brushing aside watery particles, drops which would not have appeared in their eyes had they met grim Death face to face. These sturdy men could face a tempest of wind, hail and snow without wincing, but yielded when encountering a storm of misery about to engulf the wife of a brother sailor. They could brave the majestic power of the Great Lakes, but shrank from a contest with human sorrow. Cherished by old friends are memories of Captains Wilson, Lundy and Sweet—their contemporaries who linger often recall their sterling character.

But the mystery remained: What vessel collided with the *Lady Elgin*?

After a time it was discovered that the schooner *Augusta* had disappeared from the lakes, no one knew where. After a further time, some six years thereafter, came from the sea-board a strange vessel named *Col. Cook*, and engaged in carrying iron ore from Marquette to Cleveland. On one occasion, at Cleveland, the *Col. Cook* was at Lafrinier's ship-yard for repairs. While undergoing such repairs the foreman of the yard discovered that the construction of the supposed foreign-built vessel was his own work; and, furthermore, that she was no other than the missing schooner *Augusta* which ran down the steamboat *Lady Elgin*. But her inhuman absconding crew were not accounted for.

The *Col. Cook* had made six voyages across the Atlantic in the lumber trade. Her hulk is now a tow-barge on the Great Lakes in the lumber trade. During the vigils of the night out on the waters, let her crew keep a sharp lookout for the ghostly specters, some two hundred in number, that hover over the craft of ghastly memory.

On the night of the 17th of August, 1864, the large hotel at Ontonagon, Lake Superior, was illuminated throughout its three stories. Among the guests were a number of men from the sea-board cities, interested in the rich copper mines in that vicinity. Associated with them were mining experts and business men of the Lake Superior region—in all, a party of about thirty bright men. Their business at Ontonagon for the time was closed. The steamboat *Sunbeam* was expected to arrive during the night, on which the party was to take passage down the lake. All were in good spirits, for the viands furnished at the hotel were noted for their excellence, and this was one of the gala nights of the booming era of Ontonagon. During the night the lights of the *Sunbeam* were sighted, the prepared bonfire on the beach was lighted, and soon after the steamboat was anchored off shore. At daybreak all passengers were on board, and the boat started on her passage down the lake, and six hours later the steamboat *Sunbeam* and every soul on board, were at the bottom of Lake Superior, entombed under one hundred fathoms of the coldest lake water on the globe, and where each and every victim yet remains. There is no resurrection there—the water of Lake Superior never gives up its dead.

On that fatal day an immense vacuous space must have suddenly occurred in the southeast. Never before or since has the air been known to move over Lake Superior with equal velocity. The frail steamboat *Sunbeam* was wholly unequal to the contest. To safely encounter such a tempest her unfortunate passengers and crew might as well have taken passage on a hoop-skirt.

To counteract the solemnity of melancholy reading, a humorous incident of the navigation of Lake Superior is here related.

Prior to the opening of the Soo Canal the propellers *Manhattan* and *Monticello* were conveyed overland to Lake Superior. On a day when no other boats were on the lake, in day-time and clear weather, when four miles off shore, where the lake is one hundred and fifty miles wide, they met and collided. Both boats were compelled to make for the shore, where their wrecks still remain buried in the sand. This rare feat was a consolation to canal boatmen—that they were not classed as mariners.

In 1841, the first propeller steamer known to the lakes, was, under the auspices of the inventor of the screw-wheel. Captain Ericsson, built at Oswego, by Capt. James

Van Cleve. Prior to the Oswego boat, a propeller had been built at New York, and when examining that vessel, Captain Van Cleve entered into an arrangement with the inventor to build a propeller for the lakes, and to exhibit her at the principal lake ports—hence the *Vandalia*, the original lake propeller. Under the command of Capt. Rufus Hawkins, the *Vandalia* made a trial trip on Lake Ontario, November, 1841, and the working of the screw-wheel was pronounced a success.

THE PROPELLER VANDALIA—1842.
FIRST PROPELLER ON THE LAKES.

In May, 1842, the *Vandalia* made the passage of the Welland Canal to Lake Erie, and at Buffalo was inspected with curiosity and interest by lake transporters and navigators, her advantages being explained by Captain Ericsson in person. Then, by the Hollisters, owners of the steamboats *St. Louis* and *Sandusky,* an arrangement was made to build two propellers, and the next season appeared in commission the propeller *Hercules*, Capt. F. S. Wheeler, and the *Sampson*, Capt. Amos Pratt, and both were placed as freighters in trade with Lake Michigan ports. In 1844 appeared another propeller, constructed by the Hollisters—the upper cabin passenger propeller *Princeton*, commanded by Capt. Amos Pratt. Comparatively, the *Princeton* was a modern constructed vessel, and a success. But, as a rule, lake navigators did not readily take to the propeller, and not until the middle fifties, when the railroads had paralleled the shores of the lakes, and relegated into inactivity the side-wheel passenger steamer, did the propeller come into universal use on the lakes.

The prejudice against the propeller was well illustrated when Capt. Fred S. Miller refused one as a gift. For several seasons F. S. Miller had sailed as mate with Capt. Levi Allen, while nursing the hope that his thrifty brother, Capt. W. T. Miller, would acquire the requisite interest in some side-wheeler to make him the master thereof. About 1846, Capt. W. T. Miller became possessed of a propeller, when he said to his brother Fred, that he could take and run her on his own account. But the generous offer was promptly declined, and in a manner emphatic. "I want to say to you, Captain Miller, that I am mate of the steamboat *Niagara*, and don't propose to abandon that position to be master of a thing like that." For several years thereafter, "I want to say to you, Captain Miller," was an expression frequent among lake men, until worn out. However, the marked superiority of the propeller for deep water navigation was soon acknowledged throughout the civilized world.

Fleets of grain and lumber-laden sail vessels began to make the passage of the straits, connecting Lakes Huron and Erie, in the early forties. The delays incident to such passages, caused by adverse winds, suggested a system of towing between the lakes, and for such purpose the small side-wheel steamboats, then plentiful, were utilized for towing through the rivers Detroit and St. Clair.

In the meantime the screw-wheel had demonstrated its superior power, and the more wieldy boat, with power applied under the stern, hence the screw-wheel tug-boat—now universal in waters of civilization.

Harbor towing, as an industry, was not inaugurated under favorable auspices, as at first its progress was slow. When in port vessel men were chary of a tug, fearing damage to themselves, or of causing it to others when moving about with their lines aboard. When becalmed on the lake, they were glad to be towed to the entrance of the harbor, where they would drop the tug, run their lines and warp the vessel to the dock or elevator. The first lake harbor towing was in Buffalo Creek, in 1852. During the winter of 1851-2, four screw-wheel tug-boats were under construction at Buffalo, all of which were placed in commission during the season of 1852. First to appear was the *George W. Tifft*, in June, owned by Elias and Thomas Simms, the latter her navigator. Length, 75 feet; beam, 16 feet; depth, 7 feet.

However, the *Tifft* was not the original screw-wheel tug-boat of the lakes. In 1851, the propeller tug *Franklin* was built at Albany, and upon the opening of the Erie Canal, in the spring of 1852, she made the passage of the canal to Buffalo, arriving there prior to the first of June, and at once commenced towing in Buffalo Creek, two weeks prior to the appearance of the *George W. Tifft*.

To skillfully manage a tug-boat in close quarters requires the hand and brain of an expert. Prompt action and a level head alone will often prevent disaster. The law makes the operator liable in cases of malpractice.

The tug-boat is distinguished as a life and property saver. Often has it given timely aid in places difficult and dangerous—when a life was rescued, or property saved from loss. The tug-boat captain is honored by the supposition that he and his boat are equal to any emergency, and usually they fill the bill.

An Episode.

In 1866, the tug-boat *Joe D. Dudley* was stationed at Marquette. When November came, the Soo River tugs, in order to share a rush of business on the river St. Clair, abandoned the late fleet of Lake Superior. Vessels had to make their way to Lake Huron the best they could. The ore shippers at Marquette gave inducement for the *Dudley* to go to the Soo and tow the abandoned vessels through the river to Lake Huron. December came when all but two of the fleet had passed down—the schooners *Reindeer* and *William Shupe* being still above the canal. On the third day of December the *Dudley* passed up the river to the canal in the midst of a violent storm of wind and snow, continuous for forty-eight hours. On the early morning of the fifth the *Dudley* left the canal in search of the belated vessels, with misgivings as to their fate. However, when rounding Point Aux Pins, the schooners were sighted, rolling at their anchors below Point Iroquois. The tug went alongside of the *Shupe* and found her crew heaving up anchors while treading a coating of ice overspreading the deck of the vessel—in fact, all above water-line was ice-bound. Then the tug pointed for the *Reindeer* with a view of tailing her to the *Shupe*. The little schooner presented a weird scene of frigid desolation. There she hung to her cables, responding to the roll of a heavy sea, and without a sail lowered—all hanging in frozen tatters. All in sight was ice-bound, and not a human soul in evidence, and the sounding of the whistle for a time failed to produce life. The roll of the vessel made the boarding thereof extremely difficult. Finally a man was placed aboard, just as a human head peered above the cabin hatchway—the most unkempt head imaginable—the head of Capt. Redmond Rider, and which gave voice inquisitively, "What do you want?" Darkness covered the waters when the schooners were towed into the canal, a well-remembered day of toilsome work for the crews of vessels and tug. On December 6th the *Shupe* was towed to Lake Huron, while the *Reindeer* remained at the Soo, presumably for the winter. There new sails were made, when the vessel was sailed to Detroit, directed by an intrepid man who knew not fear.

Five years later, Redmond Rider, with his command, the propeller *R. G. Coburn* went to the bottom of Lake Huron, there to join his brother, who had preceeded him a couple of years to a watery sepulcher in the same section of the lake, and where they are together entombed under forty fathoms of water. The Rider brothers were widely known among lake sailors, were considered typical seamen, noted for their intrepidity and unostentatious demeanor.

CHAPTER VIII.

During the concluding year of the village era, Dibdell Holt was publicly executed, November, 1831, for killing his wife, and his was the last public execution in Buffalo. On this occasion the gallows was erected at the junction of Genesee street and the Terrace. In Holt's case the fact was noted that he first came to Buffalo from a distance with the throng who came to witness the hanging of the three Thayers. Six years later he was the star performer in a like tragedy, presented on the same stage, and to many who were of the same audience, marching in procession over the identical ground traversed by the famous culprits whose execution his curiosity to witness was the precursor of his own doom.

While in Buffalo, in 1825, Holt became impressed with the glowing prospects of the town, remaining there several days prospecting for a location. He returned to his home, married, and at once settled in Buffalo. Being possessed of a sum of money, he purchased a lot and store thereon, on the west side of Main, a few doors above Court street, in which he established a grocery, his residence being in the story above. During the first three years of his residence in Buffalo, Holt was considered a model husband, living happily with his wife, but, contracting intemperate habits, he became sullen and morose, then cross and abusive to his wife. Her reproaches for his increasing intemperance often produced ruptures between them, when he would assure her that her days were numbered; that she would never attend his funeral, and like assertions. The day before the murder he dismissed his clerk, and closed his store. His confession after conviction discloses that he went into the room where she was sitting with their child in her arms, and while driving a nail in the wall near the ceiling, a miss-stroke caught his thumb, and at his outcry, caused by pain, she snickered, whereupon he struck her three blows on the head with the hammer, intending to kill her, which he did almost instantly. Holt then fled, meeting the servant girl on the stairs, who gave alarm, and the fugitive was pursued to the outskirts of the village, where he was found secreted in a log and brush heap, where now is Day's Park, and placed in jail. When confronted with his victim, he said that the inquest was useless ceremony, that he killed his wife, and that she deserved killing. For committing the ghastly deed. Holt deserved greater punishment than he received.

The locomotive first appeared in Buffalo in 1836, running to and from Niagara Falls. The next railroad to enter the town was the Buffalo and Attica, in 1842. Prior to the railroads, the four-horse stage coach ran out of the city on all routes. An old time advertisement reads thus:

COACH LINES.

The Pilot Mail Coach.

Leaves Buffalo every evening, arriving at Geneva the first day, Utica the second, and Albany the third.

The Diligence Coach.

Leaves Buffalo every morning at 8 o'clock, arrives at Avon the first night, Auburn the second, Utica the third, and Albany the fourth.

The Lewiston Coach.

Via the Falls. Leaves Buffalo every morning at 6 o'clock, arriving at Lewiston 7.30 p. m.

The Canada Coach.

For the Falls. Leaves every morning at 8 o'clock, arriving at the Falls at Noon. Extras furnished on either side of the river at any hour.

The Western Mail Coach.

For Fredonia, Erie and Cleveland. Leaves Buffalo every morning at 5 o'clock. Baggage at risk of the owners.

Bela D. Coe, and others.
Buffalo, March, 1828.   E. L. Stevenson, Agent.

Such were the conveniences of travel out of Buffalo sixty years ago—four days in a stage to Albany, now six hours in a luxurious car, and many passengers are impatient if there be a half-hour's detention. And such is favored human nature.

Here is an advertisement published in a local newspaper of 1828:

For Sale.—A farm in the immediate vicinity, one-half mile from the court-house, situated between two public roads, one of which will unquestionably be adopted as the Great National Road between

Buffalo and Washington. Of the premises there are about fifty-three acres, clear and stumpless, and producing good crops. Thereon is a good house and barn, and as good a spring of water as any in the country, and also $700 worth of good post and rail fence.

JOHN G. CAMP.

BUFFALO, SEPT., 1828.

The "farm" now comprises the realty bounded by Main, North, Delaware and Virginia streets. The spring of water referred to was located on the southwest corner of the tract, and is yet in evidence in the rear of the line of dwellings on Delaware avenue and Virginia street, covered by a dilapidated old framework. Around this spring, under the shade of majestic elms, were wont to camp the Indians of the vicinity, even unto the time of the advent of the city.

In 1828 there appeared at New York City a conspicuous character named Sam Patch, who subsequently became notorious in Buffalo and throughout Western New York. Sam possessed an inordinate desire for public notoriety, and, to gain such distinction, he risked life and limb in jumping from the mastheads of anchored ships into the waters of the North River. Such exploits of Sam Patch aroused the covetiveness of public purveyors who profit by the assemblage of people *en masse,* prominently the hotel and shop-keepers at Niagara Falls.

In September, 1829, it was announced far and wide that Sam Patch would jump the Niagara Falls, and then throughout the surrounding country the scheme was the general topic of conversation, the many incredulous scoffing at its absurdity. That Sam Patch had jumped from a height into the still waters of the North River was admitted, but that he would attempt a dive into the maelstrom of Niagara was considered an absurdity. This pronounced skepticism brought forth from the illustrious scapegrace his historic utterance "Some things can be done as well as others." This homely speech became proverbial and was quoted universally for years thereafter. However, on October 6, 1829, Sam Patch, from a staging projecting from the Biddle staircase, leaped into the comparatively still waters below. After a drop of 125 feet through the air he disappeared from view, but in due time appeared at the surface and was picked up uninjured, the hero of the hour and occasion.

On the platform, before making the leap, Sam manifested his frivolous egotism by hilariously singing a ribald verse:

> "I wish I were in Buffalo,
> Good friends along with me,
> I'd call for liquors plenty—
> > Have flowing bowls on ever side;
> Hard fortune never grieved me—
> > I am young and the world is wide."

Then placing to his lips a flask of rum he took a deep draught, and then added a couplet to his singing:

> "Good liquor in a poor man's house
> Is a pleasing thing to view."

And then he jumped, maintaining good posture while in descent.

There is a legend that Sam Patch repeated his jump at the Falls, drawing a larger crowd of witnesses than on the first occasion. However, adhering to his pronunciamento that "some things can be done as well as others," it was soon after announced that Sam would jump the Genesee Falls at Rochester, which he did, and at the same time jumped into eternity. From a platform elevated thirty feet above the brink of the cataract he leaped into the waters below, never again to rise in life. He was hilariously drunk, and in his descent he swung his arms wildly. When his body was found it was noted that both shoulder-joints were dislocated, the effect of striking the water with arms extended. Such was the rise and fall of the original of the present race of Steve Brodies.

At the close of 1831 Buffalo was a thriving village of nine thousand inhabitants, with the rapidly increasing commerce of Lake Erie promoting its growth. That a community of pioneers, impoverished by war and burdened with debt, contracted in re-establishing their homes despoiled in the conflict—the situation in 1820—should within the decade develop a frontier hamlet into an important commercial city was an achievement without a parallel—a consummation made possible through the perseverance, spirit and energy of its citizens. Granger, Forward, Townsend, Wilkeson, Coit, Allen, Tracy, Johnson, Walden, Pratt, Chapin, Marshall, Trowbridge, Austin, Potter, Miller, Barton, Barker, Bennett and Heacock, were an irresistible force in promoting public enterprise. In April, 1832, the important village became an ambitious young city.

1815.

"Here, on these ashes," the forefathers cried,
    "We'll now build a temple of trade;"
"Bravo!" cried Lake Erie, swelling with pride,
    "I'll cheerily join the parade."

1832.

The Pioneers wrought, their work was done,
    Their temple was wondrous fair;
The City entered and stood on the pedestal stone,
    And waved her cap high in the air.

From the beginning Buffalonians have ever been confidently enthusiastic in their predictions of an important future for their village and city. By its founders the infant city was christened with sublime confidence that wealth and importance awaited its early future. The predictions then made were, at the time, considered illusionary, born of unwonted enthusiasm, by other communities. At this advanced period they read like the profound statements of one who had, by Divine power, been entrusted with a foresight of the future. Appended is the writing of one of the founders of the city:

The "go-ahead" of the brave and eccentric Crockett, has become the watchword of the age. In every department of civilized life, in literature, in science, in mechanical arts, in the labors of the field, all seem to listen with delight to this spirit stirring talisman, and rush onward, with redoubled energy, to wealth and greatness. The march of mind is onward; our means of education are enlarging and extending their enlightening influences over the land; new discoveries are daily adding to the legacy of former times; the power of machinery is applied to almost every purpose of public utility or private enterprise in which speed is attained or labor performed—steamboats capable of contending with winds and tide, railroads which will soon enable the home-bred farmer to make the tour of the state in almost the time it takes to traverse his own domain.

Within the past fifty years mighty changes have been wrought in the relative importance and geographical extent of these United States—New England, once the nucleus around which gathered the hopes of our infant country—the center of strength and power, to whose arm the feeble branches of this family of republics looked for protection. But the scene is changed. The western world has been explored, new states have arisen as if by magic, and every year adds thousands to the throngs who have left their fatherland to rear their altars amidst the charms of the western wilderness.

The great channel of communication between the Eastern and Western States is fixed by Nature through the chain of lakes forming the division between the United States and the British possessions on the north. The Erie Canal affords a safe, easy, expeditious and cheap mode of travel, and for conveying heavy merchandise, and which forever must remain the principal thoroughfare. While goods can be shipped in New York and safely landed in Chicago in twelve days with only two re-shipments, it is not to be considered that merchants will seek other channels. With these advantages and prospects in view, the people of Buffalo may well be proud of their home, proud of the fame already acquired of their infant city. It has no rival—it can have none. Cities west of us may arise to wealth and importance, but they will be our tributaries; their growth our growth, their greatness our greatness—all combined furnish a fit epitome of the materials which are to make Buffalo one of the grandest cities in the Union. In the west lies a country destined to be a land of cities—a country of lakes and rivers, whose navigable waters traverse half the continent, and teeming with every agricultural production. The abundance of these must pass through our hands on its way to the sea-board, while the luxuries of the Old World will center here, thus rendering Buffalo what it may ever claim to be—the Great National Exchange.

But few of the present people of Buffalo are aware that a massive monument to Commodore Perry came very near being erected on the Terrace, where now stands the Liberty Pole. In 1832 the elated citizens of the newly incorporated city, organized a Monument Association, and a committee was appointed to erect in Buffalo a monument to Commodore Perry, the expense thereof to be supplied by popular subscription. The promises to pay were numerous and ample for the completion of the work, and the committee contracted for its construction in 1836; but the financial ruin of 1837 prevented the consummation of the enterprise, and in lieu thereof the Liberty Pole of 1838 was erected. The memorial was decorated with a representation of the proposed structure, and read as follows:

> This monument, to be erected by the citizens of Buffalo in honor of the late Com. Oliver Hazard Perry, is to be one hundred feet high, surmounted by a colossal statue of Perry fifteen feet in height. On

the sides of the pedestal, which is thirty-four feet square, are to be sculptured *relieves*, representing the battle of Lake Erie, and other prominent events in the life of the hero. The whole structure will be of American white marble, and cost $75,000. Its style will be Grecian. Its builders are Frazee and Launits, of the City of New York.

The committee comprised the following citizens:

Stephen Champlin, U. S. N., Chairman.

Reuben B. Heacock,	Benjamin Caryl,
Samuel Wilkeson,	John W. Clark,
Jacob A. Barker,	Pierre A. Barker,
Roswell W. Haskins,	Benjamin Rathbun,
James T. Homans, U. S. N.,	Alanson Palmer.
Henry R. Stagg,	

The original Eagle Street Theatre was erected in 1835, and opened to the public July 20th of that year. It stood midway of the block between Main and Washington streets, its front entrance being where now is the Eagle street entrance to the Hotel Iroquois. The side spaces, running to Main and Washington streets, were inclosed with a high-board fence. The inclosure on the Washington street side was occupied by the gas factory, where gas for the illumination of the house was manufactured—the first in Buffalo. When opened, the Buffalo theatre, in construction and appointment, was unsurpassed by any like institution in the country. Appended is its original announcement:

EAGLE STREET THEATRE.
A. BRISBANE, Proprietor.
DEAN & MCKINNEY, Lessees and Managers.

This splendid house will be opened July 20, 1835. The capacity of the building is exceeded by few in the Union. There are four tiers of boxes and a spacious pit, all furnished with comfortable seats; the three lower tiers with backs to the seats. The scenery and embellishments are of a style not surpassed by any theatre in the world. The whole is lighted by olefiant gas, manufactured on the premises. The managers are well known in Buffalo, and their efforts will be exerted to retain the kindness they have always experienced at the hands of the public. Performances every week-day night during the season.

The "season" was during the months of lake navigation. When navigation closed the theatre did likewise for the winter months.

The pit was consigned by the managers to the town boys—not the bad boys, but the good boys, who didn't die young—as their exclusive domain, and where they congregated nightly, at twenty-five cents per head, to witness Dan Marble in his masterly presentation of the "Game Cock in the Wilderness," and other specialties, not forgetting occasions when Edwin Forrest, supported by Josephine Clifton, was enacting Shakespearian tragedies. Mr. Dean was quite popular with the young people, with whom he maintained a genial familiarity. During a week of Forrest and Miss Clifton, the swells in the boxes leveled opera-glasses upon the stage, a proceeding novel to the boys in the pit, they considering the application of a spy-glass at such short range too silly for anything.

On Franklin above Chippewa street there lived a Dutch family named Snyder, in whose garden were a growth of seed cucumbers, sizeable and yellow, which, by boring lengthwise and connecting a pair of them, contrived a fair imitation of an opera-glass—good enough for four boys who entered the pit with such imitations concealed under their coats. During a scene when the glasses were focused upon the stage from the lower tier, the imitations were produced and focused in burlesque. Strange enough, this quietly-conducted proceeding aroused a violent disturbance among the hoodlums in the gallery—continuous until it caused the premature dropping of the curtain.

The Original Eagle Street Theatre—1835.

Whereupon, Mr. Dean appeared at the foot-lights, his appearance receiving the clapping of hands from the pit. But the usual smile did not beam on the countenance of Mr. Dean, it having an earnest cast. Mr. Dean began talking to the pit as a whole, reminding the boys of his friendly action in providing for their amusement and comfort, and then, fixing his eyes on the culprits sitting in a row, requested them to lay aside the disturbing elements that the performance might proceed without interruption. The kindly manner of Mr. Dean subdued the boys unto contrition, whereupon the guilty cucumbers were cast aside and order was resumed.

Performance at the theatre was suspended during the close of lake navigation, when the pit would be floored over, and which, with the stage, formed a commodious dancing arena. Here public balls were held during the winter season. On Franklin street resided a family named Postle, whose daughters were noted for their comeliness, and also as expert dancers, and who were frequent in attendance at the balls. The late Judge Talcott, then active, was usual in attendance—fond of the recreation.

At the time was clandestinely published *The Old Corporal* a weekly journal, 7 by 9 in size, which on the street met with ready sale, its columns giving high-wrought reports of scenes at the balls, and which, on an occasion, included the verse:

> "What *Tall-cuts* he made when attempting to wing,
> And an *Apostle* could waltz as if Fanny had lent her—
> Her heels for the evening to whirl in the ring."

The Old Corporal was the sensation of the town, until its publishers were smoked out—a brace of printers engaged on the *Express*. The veteran dispenser of billiards, Darwin

A. Slaght, was then an expert typo, and a co-perpetrator. His present sedate presentment denies the impeachment. Perish the thought!

In the fall of 1839, a full year prior to the election, a Whig National Convention assembled at Harrisburg, Pa., and nominated presidential candidates: William Henry Harrison, for President, and John Tyler, for Vice-President. In May, 1840, a Democratic National Convention convened at Baltimore, Md., where Martin Van Buren was nominated for re-election as President. Subsequently the Democratic National Committee placed Richard M. Johnson on their ticket for Vice-President, and then the trouble commenced—the log-cabin, hard-cider, coon-skin campaign for Tippecanoe and Tyler too—and the fur flew and the liquid flowed until the closing of the polls in November.

It was really a picnic campaign, a season of festivity, revelry and song, whereby General Harrison was virtually sung into the White House. Apparently, the chief issue involved was the oft-repeated inquiry: "What has caused this great commotion—motion—motion—the country through?" and which the singers themselves invariably answered in another line: "It is the ball a rolling on for Tippecanoe and Tyler too;" and to which in gracious assurance to their opponents they added: "And with them we'll beat little Van—Van, Van is a used-up man." The song was universal, like marching through Georgia, sung by marching thousands of men, women and children. The center of gravity for the Whig campaigners of Buffalo was the "Log Cabin," located for the time on the then vacant lot on the northeast corner of Main and Eagle streets. The cabin was a typical back-woods structure, the exterior decorated with grub-hoes, brush-hooks, ox-yokes, hanging scythes, gourds, crooked-necked squashes, bunches of corn-in-the-ear, coon-skins nailed on flesh-side out, and other articles traditional to pioneer industry. At the Log Cabin open house to all comers was maintained during the canvass—barrels of cider constantly on tap, and open barrels of apples, gratis to all who would join the chorus. We boys would gather at the cabin to hear the great crowd of men there assembled sing:

> "The beautiful girls, God bless their souls—
> Souls—souls—the country through;
> They will to a man do all they can
> For Tippecanoe and Tyler too."

The incongruity in the third line impressed the verse upon my youthful simplicity, permanent in memory for the half century and more intervening.

The Buffalo Historical Society preserves a faithful presentment of the historic Log Cabin.

In point of numbers in attendance, and in its varied and unique features, the Whig Mass Meeting at Buffalo, November 7, 1840, was the most notable political gathering that ever before assembled in Western New York. The celebration of the "Battle of the Thames," with their candidate the alleged hero, brought to Buffalo nearly all the adult male population of the surrounding country. Thousands came in steamboat-loads from the southern borders of Lake Erie. Buffalo, then a presumptive little city, tripled its population in a day, and its territory was not sufficient to contain the long processions marching behind bands of music, extending into the adjoining towns of Black Rock and Cheektowaga. The common rendezvous and rostrums for the meeting were on the commons south of High street, where now are rows of residences on

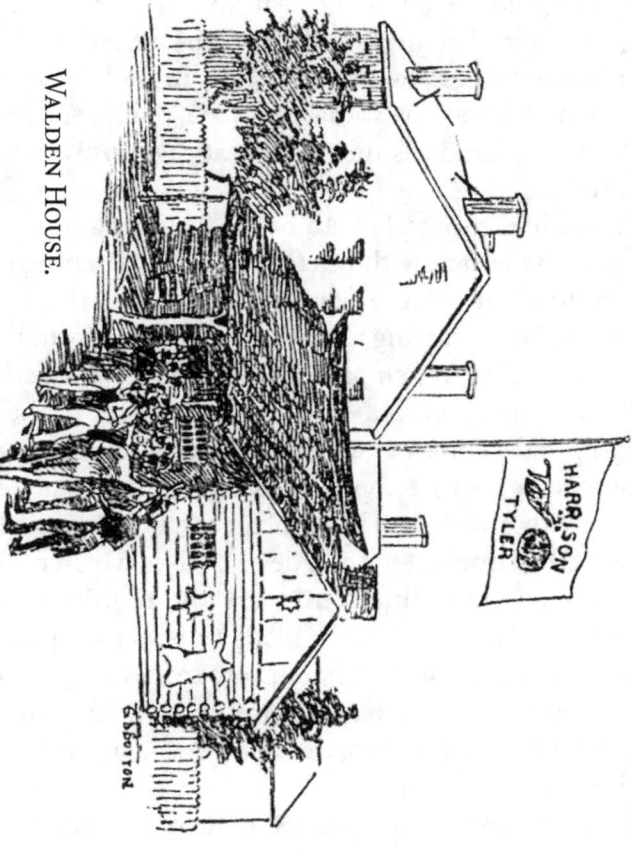

Walden House.

Northeast Corner Main and Eagle Streets—1840.

upper Oak, Elm and Michigan streets. Thomas C. Love was president of the day, assisted by numerous vice-presidents, among whom were Seth C. Hawley, Edwin Hurlbut, Daniel Bowen, Clark Robinson, C. C. Haddock and Warren Granger. Dr. Haddock was appointed Postmaster of Buffalo the following year. In 1849, when performing his duty as chairman of the Board of Health, he was stricken with cholera, then epidemic in Buffalo, and died. Dr. Haddock was an estimable citizen, public-spirited and enterprising, and his untimely death was universally regretted.

At daybreak, on a Fourth of July morning in the early forties, the writer, with other boys, was hastening downtown, to Court House Square (Lafayette Park), there to celebrate by extracting all the noise possible from the festive firecracker. When passing through Mohawk street to Washington street, on the sidewalk in front of the Congregational Church, we saw two negroes engaged in a loud quarrel. As we approached one of them stabbed the other with a dirk-knife, the blade penetrating his heart. The victim dropped to the sidewalk, over which his blood streamed to the gutter. This was the murder of James Massey by John Davis, for which Davis was hanged in the yard of the old jail, a stone's throw from the scene of his crime, and simultaneously from the scaffold with McElroy, who murdered Rapp, the German farmer, in the town of Boston.

The first cross-walk laid in Buffalo was across Main street, midway between the Terrace and Seneca, in 1828, by Josiah Beardsley. The first pavement was laid in 1836, on Main corner of Erie street, Benjamin Rathbun ordering it laid as a sample. It consisted of wooden blocks, nine inches square, which extended up about half-way across

Erie street and half-way across Main street. This block of pavement was for several years thereafter an oasis in a sea of mud, prevalent during spring and fall.

Older citizens of Buffalo will recall the municipal sun-dial, erected on Main street, west side, between Church and Niagara streets. It was a structure difficult to describe, looking more like a huge inverted plow than anything else, and not much like that. The thing was daubed over with hieroglyphics, as if of Egyptian origin, lined with marks and counter-marks to allow the sun to cast shades and reveal the hour of day to the astronomically educated. It was of but little use to them, and of no use whatever to anyone else. However, it was the source of amusement to many, being subjected to the jests of the fun-makers of the town at the expense of the Board of Aldermen, who ordered its construction at the cost of the tax-payers to the amount of several hundred dollars. It had not been in place a week before the all-around wag, Fred Emmons, had a farmer's load of hay alongside to be weighed at a reduced price. Fred made application to be appointed Keeper of the Sun Dial, unrolling before the aldermen in session a "universal petition," both sides filled with names, consisting of the city directory, the leaves cut out and connected lengthwise. His memorial promised that over the dial would be erected a shed to protect it from the sun! Finally, under the darkness of night, the "what-was-it" escaped, probably, aided by its projectors. The Historical Society should endeavor to discover its hiding-place. It has nothing more facetiously or curiously historic.

"Not since the flood," was an expression often used by Buffalonians when citing a time remote. Not to the downpour of Scripture did they refer, but to the disastrous inflow of the waters of Lake Erie upon the lower lands of Buffalo, October 18, 1844. To those participating in these historic events, the local flood was the less considerate, giving no warning to its victims, but instead an unheralded avalanche of waters came upon a sleeping community, the howling tempest arousing them from their slumbers like the sound of a fire-bell at night. For three days previous to the flood of waters, a northeast wind had been continuous, driving the waters of the lake upwards, when the wind suddenly shifted to the opposite direction with tremendous force, bringing with it a flood of waters to the foot of the lake, greater than ever before or since known, inundating the lower districts of Buffalo, demolishing scores of dwellings and other buildings, spreading ruin along the harbor front, playing havoc with the shipping, and causing great destruction of life. Not until the night of the 19th did the gale abate its velocity, and the waters recede. The rise of water can be imagined from the fact that before the blow the steamboat *Columbus* was aground in the river at the foot of Indiana street, and when the waters receded the steamboat was left behind on Ohio street.

The adult male population of the city were active in the rescue of the imperiled and providing relief for the suffering during the early morning and through the day. The municipal hall over the Terrace Market was thronged with agonized people scanning bodies of the drowned as they were brought in, fearfully expectant of discovering missing friends whom they hoped might be somewhere in life. A like scene was at the court-house, where the bodies of the dead lay in rows awaiting identification. There strong men were moaning over the inanimate bodies of wives and children, while mothers and children were weeping over the dead bodies of male members of their families.

In the memory of the writer the arrival of that terrific first blast of wind remains vivid. He was sleeping in the upper room of a house then and now standing on North Main street, in a room comprising the length and breadth of the front portion of the house. The first blast carried the sash of the west end window bodily against the east wall of the room near the head of the bed, shattering the glass into a thousand fragments. He has ever since been unable to recall his sensation on being thus violently awakened, other than a vague realization of kingdom come—something of that import.

Men who saw the initial wave invade lower Main and Commercial streets, stated that it rolled up and poured into the canal with roaring sound. At the corner of Main and Ohio streets there was a depth of six feet of water, and of four feet at Exchange and Michigan streets. All territory on the level of outer Exchange street was alike inundated. Many harbor craft were left distant from their element when the waters receded. The flat lands southeast of the city were strewn with wreckage. For the second time the steamboats *Columbus* and *Chautauqua* required launching into the waters of the lake. Published details told of many providential escapes and timely rescues. Over the river near the ship-yard were two families, each consisting of parents and one child, living in houses adjoining. To escape the rising waters, both families took refuge on the roof of the stancher building, where they saw the other crumble and float away with all it contained. Soon after the house on which they were perched collapsed and floated off with the flood, the six human souls clinging to the floating roof. Not until seven o'clock that morning were they taken off their raft by rescuers in yawl-boats, and after floating more than a mile away on a frail float amid the rush of waters and howling tempest.

M. W. Dayton, brother of the ex-mayor, with his family, resided in a cottage on South Division street, his house standing alongside of a new three-story brick structure then under construction. Becoming alarmed at the rattling of falling *debris* upon the roof of his house, Mr. Dayton aroused his family to take them to a place of safety. Just as they passed out the front gate, the brick wall fell upon and crushed the cottage.

A. S. Carpenter and family were taken into a boat from the garret window of their dwelling on Jackson street in the early morning, just in time to save them from a collapsed building and floating wreckage. The evening before the great blow, the steamboats *Saint Louis*, *Robert Fulton*, *Juliet Palmer*, *Chautauqua*, and *Indian Queen*, left Buffalo with their usual complement of passengers. The *Saint Louis* encountered the tempest abreast of Dunkirk, and when essaying to breast it, broke her shaft, and, paying into the troughs of the sea, four men were washed overboard and lost. Aided by a stay-sail and jib, the steamer drifted before the wind and was carried down Niagara River, when Captain Haggart, with his ferry boat, came and assisted the disabled steamer to a landing at the foot of Ferry street.

After having three people washed overboard, the steamboat *Robert Fulton* was piled upon the beach above Stony Point. The *Chautauqua* was driven high and dry on the sand beach at the foot of Hudson street.

The *Indian Queen*, a bonnie little steamboat, was the only one of the outgoing fleet that succeeded in making Buffalo harbor on their return. Like a hog in a mire, she came wallowing in the huge seas directly to its entrance.

The *Julia Palmer*, with her three hundred passengers, was blown helplessly down the lake to a point in the bay opposite the foot of Main street, where her anchors held, and where she pitched and rolled all the live-long day in a manner fearful to behold. On the morning of the 20th, a relief boat assisted her into the harbor, greatly to the relief of her terrorized passengers and worn-out crew.

The steamboat *Julia Palmer*, a historic vessel, built by a historic citizen, at a historic period, and named for a historic Buffalo matron, lies imbedded in the sands of a Lake Superior beach. Peace to her ashes!

CHAPTER IX.

It was an August day in 1849; Buffalo was overspread with gloom, owing to the ravage of Asiatic cholera. An alarm of fire came from the First Ward. A factory building was burning away out Perry street. In good time Fulton Fire Company No. 3 came out of West Seneca street, wheeling downward into Main street, just in time to encounter Red Jacket No. 6, and then the trouble commenced—a run to the fire. All old volunteers will recall the wild clamor attendant upon such a contest between old-time fire companies; even more exciting and picturesque than the galloping of horses through the streets of the present. On that occasion, it was a victory for No. 3 over their most active rivals in the department, and to them a cause for hilarious congratulation.

When No. 3 reached the fire, Mayor Hiram Barton was there standing in an open carriage, having been on a visit to the locality on sanitary inspection. The rear yard was inclosed with a high board fence. The mayor shouted: "Foreman Reed, can your boys jump over that fence?"

"My boys can jump over anywhere, Mr. Mayor!" was the reply of as good a fireman as was ever known to Buffalo.

Then the pipemen were lifted to where they could grasp the top, and over the fence they went, and soon two streams were penetrating the rear openings of the burning building, while with the rest of the company it was, "shake her up, boys," until the little piano engine rocked like a jolly-boat in the surf.

On the home march, it was evening twilight when No. 3 wheeled out of Perry into Main street, where, in full company, they "spread out," and all gave voice to the song of the marching firemen. On that occasion the verses were chorused thus:

> "We are the boys who can run to the front,
>   And jump over anywhere!
> It's our delight, any sort of a night,
>   All seasons of the year."

The hilarious march up the desolate street dispelled the gloom for the time, the singing bringing the people out on to the sidewalks in goodly numbers.

It was often remarked that among the residents of early Buffalo there were a number whose characteristics were remarkably peculiar. A score of such—now of the past—could be named. Among this class was John K. Tucker, the whilom proprietor of Tucker's Hotel, on Exchange street. Mr. Tucker was a rare combination of assumption and vocal energy. Mr. Tucker had other characteristics, among which was a conceit that he excelled in horsemanship. That he was a master of arts and parts of which the animal is often the subject, was generally conceded. Early during the civil war, Mr. Tucker was a contractor to supply army horses, and to him I sold a pair designed for artillery service. When paying for them, Mr. Tucker said to me, "By the way—I want to show you a good horse for you to buy." At his stables a serviceable appearing animal was led out. Mr. Tucker remarked, "This horse we bought of a farmer in Hamburg, but the inspector rejected him, because of this wind-gall on his ankle, which you know don't hurt him. We paid a hundred for him; he is in our way; take him along at eighty." After close inspection, I said to Mr. Tucker, that if the horse was a good worker I would take him. "He is all right; we have tried him," said Mr. Tucker. I then paid Mr. Tucker eighty dollars, and the horse was transferred to my stable. The next morning, when a harness was thrown upon him, he kicked viciously with both feet, and so continued to vibrate until the menial appliance was removed from his lordly presence, thus evincing that he had more gall than was contained in the puff on his ankle. Being aware that his late owner was well supplied with the bitter commodity, redress was deemed hopeless.

A few days thereafter an agent of Mr. Tucker, named Peters, arrived from Canada with a car-load of horses. Mr. Peters was then assigned to canvass the home market, with rolls of greenbacks in his pockets. It was thought a good scheme to intercept Mr. Peters. Acting on the inspiration, I was soon in his wake, and in good time sighted the buyer at the Cold Spring tavern "Hardfinish" Clark was the landlord, and with him I had a private interview, and then hastened homeward. In good time "Hardfinish" informed Mr. Peters that he knew where there was a horse for sale that would make a good mount for an army officer. Mr. Peters was interested. "Hardfinish" would locate the animal under conditions. These being arranged the worthies drove to my stable, where the horse with a wind-gall on his ankle was inspected. Mr. Peters seemed pleased, and suggested a saddle. He was informed that a saddle was not available, but that Mr. Tucker knew me, and that I would guarantee the horse a bold actor—a veritable warhorse. Mr. Peters was desirous to obtain the horse for ten dollars less than my price—one hundred dollars. Finally, Mr. Peters paid me ninety dollars and led the horse away covertly handing "Hardfinish" a ten-dollar note. The next morning Mr. Peters returned, leading the horse with a wind-gall on his ankle. Mr. Peters stated that Mr Tucker didn't want that horse. Mr. Peters further remarked that he did want me to return to him ninety dollars paid to me the day before. Mr. Peters was advised that his petition would be placed on file. He was requested to present my compliments to Mr. Tucker, and say that when having a horse he didn't want, the proper thing was to sell him if he could, but that I did not desire to purchase—not that day.

When again meeting Mr. Tucker he was agitated. His language was plain, but undignified. He seemed hurt. He had fired his battery with complacency, but the recoil disconcerted him. Mr. Tucker was reminded that man was made to mourn.

The late John Pierce, ex-Deputy Sheriff, Alderman, and Police Commissioner, possessed peculiar characteristics. To a great degree quiet and unobtrusive in manner, yet obtrusive in perpetrating jokes upon his friends, of whom there were many. Between Pierce and George B. Efner a close friendship ever existed. Both were passionately fond of animals—the horse occupying the seat of honor, and both were ever on the lookout for promising young animals at a low price, that they might develop and sell for a high price, and of this industry both were experts, skilled operators and rivals.

One day when George was alone in his stable office, John drove up, that being his horse-boarding stable. Stepping into the office and giving George a slap on the shoulder, he remarked: "George, my boy, I know where there is a slick one; he'll make your eye shine when you see him. I'm going to gather him in, too."

In the team of a farmer on the hay market John discovered a young horse that filled his eye, and at once proceeded to interview the farmer. Pointing to the mate of the fancied animal, he said: "You've a good horse there?"

"Yes," said the farmer, "she's a good old mare. Do you want to buy a horse?"

"No," said John, "but I like to look at 'em."

"Take a look at the one on the other side," said the farmer.

The more John looked at him the better he liked him. "He looks fairly well," said John.

"Yes, he's an extra good colt, and if a man wants to buy, I'll sell cheap, for I must raise some money," said the farmer.

"What do you hold him at?" said John.

"One hundred and forty dollars will buy him," said the farmer.

John answered this with a significant whistle. In a manner unconcerned, John stepped aside, but soon after casually offered one hundred dollars for the colt, which offer the farmer declined to accept, and then this acute interview ended. After finding out from another farmer where "that man lived," John drove to Efner's, when the scene before related occurred.

That night the farmer's colt haunted John's sleep, and the next day he thought of some business he *didn't* have in the town of Alden, where lived the farmer who had a horse whose owner John considered failed to appreciate his full value. The next morning a couple of hours' drive brought John Pierce to a farm house in Alden, where he halted, ostensibly to make an inquiry. There John was surprised to find the owner of the young horse that he had "no use for, but liked to look at." After some irrelevant talk, the farmer brought the colt out to show Mr. Pierce his action when turned loose in a paddock. The exhibition increased John's admiration for the animal. Finally he renewed his offer of one hundred dollars for him.

"Can't sell him for that, but I want money, and you can take him for $125," said Mr. Brown.

John shook his head, as he walked slowly to where his horse stood, but faced about and offered to split the difference.

"Can't hardly do that," said Mr. Brown.

Then John entered his buggy and started off slowly, feeling assured that he would be called back; but the call came not, and John drove home feeling sorry that he was not leading the coveted colt which he had determined to buy in any event.

At Efner's stable, the next morning, John said to George: "George, my boy, I am going to Lockport to-day, but to-morrow I'm going for the horse I told you about. My mare is a little lame, and the road is rather heavy. You have a pair hooked up for me early in the morning, and when I return will show you something that will please you."

Soon after a load of hay was driven to Efner's stable to be unloaded. The man with the hay said to Efner:

"Who was that man talking to you when I drove up?"

"Why, that was John Pierce, the deputy sheriff, don't you know him?"

"No; but I saw him out our way yesterday trying to buy a horse of my neighbor, Mr. Brown, but they couldn't make a trade."

Then George was interested.

"What sort of a horse is it?"

"Mighty good colt, I tell you, best one in our town."

This information was nuts and wine for Efner, and soon after he was on his way to Alden, and that evening he placed a young horse that formerly belonged to farmer Brown, in a stall of his stable—his property. The next morning John promptly appeared, the team was ready, and off he went after Mr. Brown's colt. On his arrival Mr. Brown was in front of his house.

"Good morning," said John.

"Good morning, Sheriff," said Mr. Brown.

"Mr. Brown, I've concluded to take the colt at your figure. Here's your money, and here's a leading-bridle to put on him," said Mr. Pierce.

"What are you driving at?" said the farmer.

"Why, you've got the horse there, on the off side. Mr. Efner was out here yesterday and bought him."

For the moment John Pierce was stunned, and when he regained his breath he ejaculated, "Holy Ghost!" then applying the whip, the horses shot out as if answering a fire-alarm. On the way home John was unable to solve a conundrum by himself propounded: "How in hades did George Efner learn of that horse?" When John reached the city it occurred to him that his business down-town was not pressing, so he gave the team to a policeman to drive to Efner's stable. When the friends next met George asked:

"John, didn't you get the horse? "

"No," said John. "I discovered a nice little spavin growing on his hind leg, and made up my mind that John Pierce didn't want him."

"Ah, ha! smarty. You had better get that spavin out of your eye, it might lame you," replied George.

Many old Buffalonians will recall a quiet, cross-eyed little sport named Isaiah Smith, who was wont to parade the streets, twirling his cane. Occasionally Isaiah would drop into the saloon on West Huron street, kept by George Sherwood, the well-known singer, police constable and horseman. On the end of the counter stood a glass globe, nearly filled with water, the home of two little gold-fish. The door stood open one day, when Isaiah softly stepped in and peeked into the glass globe. Taking the tail of a fish between his thumb and finger, he raised and deftly dropped the tiny creature into his mouth, and down his throat it went. Observing the disappearance of his pet fish, Sherwood said, angrily: "You had better swallow the other one." No sooner said than done, when Isaiah coolly lit a cigar and passed out, twirling his cane as he went. Sherwood was mad as a wet hen, but said nothing more to Isaiah, he being quite handy with the pistol when attacked. In partaking of the free lunch not a word was uttered by the luncher.

During the decade of the thirties, before telegraph lines were known, horse-stealing was reduced to a science in Western New York. Appropriating and running animals over the Niagara into Canada, was an industry successfully prosecuted by bold operators, whose frequent depredations were such a burden and annoyance to the citizens, that protective associations were organized in the several communities, consisting of troops of mounted men, to pursue and recover stolen horses, and capture the thieves.

These companies held themselves in readiness for duty at the call of their commander, in the manner of the historic "minute men," all superbly mounted, and otherwise well found for continuous pursuit. However, these troopers were often unsuccessful in their pursuits, in coping with the cunning thieves, who, fox-like, had convenient holes of refuge by day, then to flee the country by night. The pursued held the advantage of their pursuers in being familiar with the routes taken, thus enabling a flight unobserved by sleeping communities; in being well mounted, as superior animals only were by them appropriated, all of which facilitated escape. Thus trails were lost and captures prevented.

The local troop was a superior organization, exceptionally well mounted, and otherwise equipped for efficient service. The following were among the number: Samuel R. Atkins, of Buffalo Plains, commander: William C. Brown, William Holt and Samuel Eley, of Buffalo Plains; John S. King, Adam Rinewalt and T. S. Hopkins, of Amherst; William Wire and Jacob Schell, of Tonawanda; Michael Shultz, Vincent Rogers and James Saddler, of Clarence.

The writer recalls a dress parade of this troop on Buffalo Plains and the admiration he had for the array of cavaliers, their equipment and evolutions.

A short time after the parade, a paradoxical event occurred, the theft of a valuable pair of mares from the commander of the troop, which were not recovered, notwithstanding the country was traversed far and wide in their pursuit. Not a trace was obtained of horses or thieves beyond LeRoy, where they breakfasted the morning after the theft. The perpetrators of the bold venture were a brace of experts named Ambrose and Joe Bois. When at home the Bois brothers were at the house of their mother in Buffalo, on the north side of Court street, between Main and Pearl streets.

Five years later, January, 1840, the sheriff was advised that Ambrose Bois was secretly visiting his mother and measures were taken for his arrest. He was known to be a desperate character when at bay, and due precaution was observed. A watch was placed on the house, and when night came a raid was made and the culprit captured and placed in jail. At the March Term of Oyer and Terminer he was convicted of the theft and sentenced to five years at Auburn. Joe Bois evaded arrest for this crime, but in gracious compensation ended his life in the Ohio penitentiary.

Speeding horses on the snow-path was an old-time winter amusement in Buffalo. The scenes attendant on early occasions, first on Main and then on Delaware street, are now repeated on Richmond Avenue. New Year's Day in ye olden time was celebrated in social reunions—out sleighing in huge sleighs drawn by four and six horses, decorated with plumes and flags, which, together with hundreds of smaller turn-outs, constituted a carnival of good cheer—a day of jubilee. But the actors in the old comedies have in the main disappeared. Modern actors may be interested in the rehearsal of a scene presented on Delaware avenue forty-live years ago:

Time, January 1, 1854.

The writer, with horse and sleigh at Main and Seneca streets, espies an acquaintance on the walk, a resident of an adjacent village, hurrying up-town.

"Hello, George! Whither are you drifting?"

"Going up to Stevenson's to get a rig—want to see the trotters."

"Just so. Get in here under this robe, I'll show you the circus."

"All right. Here I am; now proceed. But we'll need some cigars. Pull up at Boas's and I'll skip in and get some."

The cigars were lighted and the drive was to Niagara Square, where we found Delaware avenue filled with turnouts.

"Here we are in the midst of them. Now we'll join the procession and see how people enjoy cold feet and blue noses."

My companion was all observant.

"That's a nice old gentleman with that big chestnut, who's he?"

"That's Jacob S. Miller and 'Old Captain'—man and horse—both are captains."

"Jerush! That's a nobby establishment, horses and sleigh, with colored plumes."

"Yes; that's A. D. Patchin, the banker. The large man on the rear seat is Asa B. Meech. Both have the horse distemper."

"Here's a fine horse. Who's the driver with fur cap, collar and gloves?"

"That's Chandler Wells; he, too, has the disease."

"That's a fine pair—that sorrel and black, hooked up light. Who's the airy chap driving?"

"Oh, that's West India Mills. But the horses are all right—'William T. Porter' and 'Belle of Saratoga.' They can road a thirty clip. The man in furs with the brown mare is Frederick Gridley, the broker. The man and wife in the Portland are Mr. and Mrs. Arthur Fox. The lady is the daughter of a horseman and inherits admiration for the animal."

"Who are those larks?"

"Walter Harris and George Coburn, and the mare is the trotter 'Knownothing.' Wait till you see them pass through with the gang. It will make you hold your cap on."

"That gray pacer is a dandy. And so are the two sports in the cutter, I should say."

"You've guessed it. That's Cart Sawin and Ed. Blancan. Their gray pony can melt the snow when set going. The man in the plain cutter is Jay Pettibone, the distiller. His horse is liable to be speedy. That tandem? Why, that's Doctor Cary, and he enjoys it."

"Who's the fat old chap on the rear seat of that hack sleigh?"

"That's Charles Norton, Buffalo's Jack Falstaff."

"He looks as if he loved sack."

"You bet."

"That yellow bay is a good stepper, and I reckon the driver is another."

"Yes, yes, right you are. That's Lanse Thomas and 'Canary Bird.' When she sings he jigs."

"Can he dance?"

"Dance! It would make you shed tears to see him sing and dance 'Uncle Snow':"

> "My name is Uncle Snow, I have you all to know,
> I's de slickest wid de brush in all creation;
> I's gwine down to Washington to take a little job,
> To whitewash all de free nigs in de nation."

"Who's the Russian turn-out?"

"That's Goodenough, the Exchange-street broker; and the man alongside is Tom Smith, the bonnet dealer. Smith loves his horse, but can't hear him cough when he has a cold. There comes O. W. Dimock with 'Jack Rositer,' the champion two-miler. Otis won't speed him in the street. Has brought him out for an airing. He's a trotter that can burn the track from the half to the wire. And there comes George Hosley with 'Tib Hinman.' George won't speed with the brigade. The little mare is too sweet to take such chances. Yes, she's a trotter. Got a record on the ice at Ogdensburg of 2.22."

"That gray is moving nicely. Who's the driver?"

"That's Judge Masten, with 'Recorder.' He has two or three good ones in his stable. Now, we have made the circuit. The brigade are congregating at Virginia street for the down drive, and we'll soon see some fun."

"Yes; and here come three of them. Look out!"

"They are moving well. The leader is Lyman B. Smith, with his trotter 'Fred,' and on his quarter is Harvey Peek, with his Arabian spike, and George Malcom, close up."

"Malcom! Is he the Cold Spring distiller?"

"Yes; and he's a trotter, too. Thinks more of them than of getting a wife."

"And here they come! Jehu! See the snow fly."

"Yes, yes; they are the boys to stir up the snow. The leader is W. W. Huff, the horse doctor, with the trotter 'Mayflower.' Next, and close up, is Edwin Hurlbut, with the 'Hurlbut Mare,' and right up with them is Peter Young driving the 'Patrick Pony,' now called 'Acorn'. Next to Peter is Lauren Burton, with 'Black Maria,' and lapped onto Burton is George Efner, driving 'Mary Blane'—no better roadster anywhere, and she can trot, too, as you observe."

"Here comes another bunch of them."

"Yes; the rest of the gang: Pop Horter, George Harris, Eli Boyington, William Lockwood, Fordyce Cowing, Forman Mount, Wooster Burton, and in the rear, his usual place, is George Metzger with 'Missouri'. And there comes John Stevenson with the six-horse sleigh and a full cargo of web-footers. There are Captains Fred Wheeler, Peter Smith, Bill Stone, Jim Snow, T. J. Titus, Bill Arthur, Fred Miller, Bob Wagstaff, Jim Beckwith, Jim Hathaway, Amasa Kingman, Luther Chamberlain and Harry Watts, all lake captains, and with them are their two landsmen chums. Deacon Alvord and Gust. Tiffany. That party will paint the town before midnight."

"And there's another six-horse turn-out."

"Yes; that's the American Express Company's sleigh. Let us see who compose the party. There is W. G. Fargo, W. B. Peck, A. G. C. Cochrane, Jacob Dygert and Ham. Best, all of the company, and their guests are Judge Verplanck, Charles Ensign, George W. Holt, Charles E. Peck, Captain E. P. Dorr, A. S. Bemis, William Kasson, George W. Bull, George P. Stevenson and T. T. Bloomer, a good lot and a fine team. See how nicely Sherman curves the leaders up Niagara street."

Now the shades of evening appeared. My companion was silent and contemplative. He recuperated in good shape:

"Say! How would a hot-scotch sit on our stomachs?"

"Soothingly."

"Well, where can we get 'em in good strength?"

"At McDougal's, on Seneca street."

"Jerush! That's a good ways. But hurry up, let the horse travel, I'm suffering."

Soon after the animal was warmly blanketed on Seneca street— ×   ×   × —three of a kind.

In the fall of 1859 a social association was organized in Buffalo, named the B. B. B. D., having a large membership, which held nightly meetings in an apartment of St. James Hall. C. C. Bristol was its president, and his onerous duties were shared by a galaxy of vice-presidents and secretaries. For the election of new members frequent executive sessions were held, when the caliber of the candidate would be voluminously discussed by the lawyers, doctors and steamboat captains, who were numerous in attendance. The initiation fee for a member, was a half bushel of pretzels (in the twist) and a keg of beer—with a renewal payment at stated intervals. The qualification for a desirable member was involved in his disposition to purchase supplies on festive occasions. The oratorical capacity, ethics and lung power concentrated in the association, was to a degree stupendous, and the complex conundrums given to the chairman to solve, were handled by President Bristol with masterly art. The owl-like wisdom displayed by him on such occasions was convulsively amusing.

The application of citizen Charles Norton for membership, caused animated discussion. Those opposed held that the applicant would be a greater consumer than a provider of viands; on the other hand it was contended that his capacity to consume would be beneficial, inasmuch as a fresh supply for each banquet would be assured in lieu of stale goods. Then a member arose and stated that he knew the applicant well, that his disposition to purchase was profound—on credit—whereupon a magnanimous brewer arose and stated that he would accord a line of credit to the applicant, when, amid applause, Mr. Norton was unanimously elected a member of the association.

During the winter the local press made frequent appeals for aid for the needy poor, when the association resolved itself into a relief organization for needy families of the city, to solicit, collect and distribute donations from the citizens at large. Wagons traversed the streets, attended by committees, who would receive donations of any character—food, clothing or furniture—and soon the commodious basement of St. James Hall was filled with commodities, and was the base of supplies for the distributing committees. On February 9, 1860, the association held a festival at St. James Hall, which was an immense success, the building and street being inadequate to hold the people who responded to the thousands of invitations distributed by the Grand Secretary, Henry W. Faxon. The circular distributed by that versatile journalist comprised, besides the invitation to attend, an invitation to donate, naming many varieties of articles which would be received, and the program for an exhibition from the stage, ending with a series of tableaux of local nature and interest. The following is the Faxon circular:

BUFFALO GRAND BENEVOLENT ASSOCIATION.

To . . . .

Sir—You are respectfully invited to attend the Annual Festival of this Association, to be held at St. James Hall, on Thursday, February 9, 1860.

Admit the Bearer.

H. W. Faxon, Chairman Committee of Arrangements.

Prelude.

Gentlemen and ladies desirous of contributing to the needy poor will find in the list herein enumerated abundant aggravation for the vacation of their pockets, the decimation of their personal property in stocks, bonds and bank notes, and other calamities. But no gentleman, it is hoped, will be so carried away by the excitement of the occasion as to donate anything that may militate against the claims of his own widows and orphans, which should be paramount to all else.

Articles Peculiarly Acceptable.

VICTUALS AND THINGS.

Charlotte Russe in packages, or Charlottes without ruse. Fresh Dutchwomen's hens' eggs. Ducks on foot, in the pond, or in the quack, if not donated by medical students. Pigs, roasted or broiled, in the pen, or in the tenderloin. Flour, in sacks and barrels, or in doughnuts. Buckwheat, with the scratch extracted. Indian and oatmeal, shorts and middlings, by the ton. Beer, in quarters, halves and wholes, by the dray load—or in the *Courier* office. Sausages, in the hog or dog, in the smooth or in the rough. No. 1 mackerel; to feed country editors, a few kits of No. 10 in the rust, will be tolerated. Ice cream, froze tight. Sugar and molasses in hogsheads. Codfish, in crates or quintals. All kinds of fish, comprehending suckers, sardines, turtle, Rochester mullet and Tonawanda bullheads. Native fruit, such as apples and protested notes of hand, by the bushel or barrel. Chickens and oysters, in the shell or on foot, in the feather or the keg, or on commission. Butter, by special contract—none strong enough to donate itself will be tolerated. Corned beef will be accepted, drunk or sober. Milk, from the cow, pump or distillery. Young and old farmers' veal, when accompanied with affidavits. Geese, with squawks and liver complaint extracted. Porter-house steaks, with the tenderloin in. In fact, any kind of victuals that can make the palate enthusiastic and the stomach jubilant.

GARMENTS.

Pea jackets, monkey jackets and water jackets. Pantaloons, with pockets mortised in. Undershirts, in muslin de laine or buckskin, or in moire antique. Drawers, of wool, cotton, slippery elm or tin foil. The variety trimmed with Brussels lace not wanted. Neckties, in silk, welting-cord or hemp. Stockings (darned), long or short. Capes, cloaks and muffs in Russian sable, seal or ermine. Buffalo-skins and balmoral skirts. Damask and other curtain goods. In fact, everything made of any kind of fibre, except the *Buffalo Express*.

LUXURIES.

After the solids, as above enumerated, the following luxuries will be especially acceptable: Gold, in bullion, bushels, bags or half bushels. Silver, in limited quantities. Gold bricks not accepted. Bills of exchange, in large amounts—on London preferred. Farmers' Joint Stock Bank notes and false teeth. Turtle shell combs and rubber overshoes. Confessions of recent murderers, and hangman's ropes, with the knot in. Counterfeit coin, by sample. Gold-rimmed eye-glasses and Pittsburg Railroad stock—the latter in limited quantities. Opera-glasses and glass eyes. Cod-liver oil and bids for city printing. Corn plasters, quinine pills and dried beef. Mathews' hair dye and salt-rheum ointment. Messenger colts and Jersey heifers, and rock and rye in large quantities.

Objects of Virtu.

Defeated candidates for mayor, and wood by the cord. Democratic majorities at the last election—if hermetically sealed. Disappointed office seekers and Powers' Greek Slaves. Sugar plums and kisses, of the tu-lip variety. Sugar-cured hams and Palmer's marbles. Members of Assembly and silk mufflers or anything else woven pliably by hand or loom. Liquors and cigars, by dray loads. Donors in this department have a wide field to operate in, and it is hoped that they will commence early and persevere in the good work, as there are many applicants for relief who have a refined taste for these goods. If there be anything you have not in the above list, why, send it in at once, and not mind the expense or consequences.

Note.

Although there is no resolution strictly forbidding the presence of ladies at the festival, the committee are of the opinion that it would be as well for them to stay at home and take care of the children.*

*But they didn't stay away worth a cent—they came in flocks.

Of the village boys, who were to the manor born, but few survive to close the century. Of the number resident in the city, Oscar F. Crary is the eldest, born in 1816. Next in point of age is Pascal P. Pratt, born in 1819. In 1823 appeared George B. Efner and Alvin D. Gilbert. Of the births of 1826, Hiram C. Day and the writer hereof remain. Washington Russell was born in 1828, and David F. Day in 1829. John E. McManus was in evidence at the close of the village era. There are resident in Buffalo a number of elderly ladies who, it is believed, were village girls, but, owing to an impediment in their memory as to their exact age, such belief cannot be verified. An exception is Miss Sabrina Hosford, of Main street, who confesses to her birth in Buffalo in 1815. Miss Hosford has witnessed Buffalo's evolution from a hamlet to a metropolis—from Red Jacket to Mayor Diehl.

With this chapter ends the sketches of early Buffalo. And it is well. Reflection recalls the admonition:

"Is not your voice broken? your wind short? your wit single? and every part of you blurred with antiquity?"

Just so, Mr. Shakespeare.

BUFFALO.

Where flaming swords were in anger drew,
Where Red Jacket paddled his canoe,
And three Thayers hanged in open view—
    Was Old-time Buffalo.

Where savage life in the main prevailed,
Where approach was by Indian trail,
Then rail-trains met the gliding sail—
    Was Progressive Buffalo.

Where Great Lakes lay their tribute down,
Where miles of handsome homes abound,
And where its people own the town—
    Is Domestic Buffalo.

Where are rural parks and cosy drives,
Where shaded lawns in beauty thrive,
And massive structures point the skies—
    Is Picturesque Buffalo.

Where Niagara flows a rapid stream,
Where Nature's power replaces steam,
And bustling streets are smooth and clean—
    Is Excelsior Buffalo.

    Let zephyrs blow, high or low—
    "Put me off at Buffalo."

APPENDIX.

From the New York Missionary Magazine of December, 1800.

FORT NIAGARA, October 29, 1800.

REVEREND AND DEAR BROTHER: Through the kind providence of God, I arrived the 14th of this month at the Seneca Castle, five miles above where the Buffaloe empties into Lake Erie. I waited on the chief sachem (called Farmer's Brother) with Cusoc, my interpreter, and made known to him my business, and asked his favor, and for the chiefs of the nation to meet me in council. He informed me that he had heard of me before, and that he would consult with the chiefs, and as soon as they could be ready he would let me know it. I then took my leave of him, leaving Cusoc to tarry in the village, and went to a village of white people, consisting of five or six families, at the mouth of the Buffaloe.

On Friday following Cusoc came and informed me that the chiefs would meet in council that afternoon and that they desired me to attend. I proceeded to the Castle, and on arrival found the sachems and chiefs, with about one hundred Indians, assembled in the Council House. Soon after I was seated, Red Jacket, the second sachem, addressed me in a short speech, complimenting me upon my arrival among them and saying that they were ready to hear what I had to say. I then arose and addressed them as I thought proper, and delivered the talk (as they style it) from the directors of the missionary society.

I left Buffaloe on Monday and reached here yesterday—in hopes of seeing my friend Major Rivardi before he left, but was two hours too late. He is removed from the command of this post. One Major Porter now commands here. I propose to be with the Tuscaroras until next month and then return to the Senecas.

* * * * *

ELKANAH HOLMES.

Rev. J. M. MASON,
Secretary of the Missionary Society, New York.

APPENDIX.

From the New York Missionary Magazine of December, 1800.

The following address was made to me by Red Jacket, Second Sachem of the Senecas, at the Council House, Seneca Castle, on the 15th day of October, 1800.

ELKANAH HOLMES.

"Father: We are happy that the Great Spirit has permitted us to meet together this day. We heard what you spoke to us. We thank the Great Spirit for putting into the minds of the good society of friendship in New York to send you to visit us. On your way to visit us you called on our brothers, the Oneidas, Muhhecomuks, and the Tuscaroras. We thank them for sending this good talk with wampum (holding the wampum up). We believe that you mean to do good to us, that there is no cheat in your talk, or in the society that sent you to us."

He then spoke to his people, charging them to make no noise and pay attention to what I had to say. I then proceeded to preach to them of Jesus Christ. When I had concluded Red Jacket arose and again addressed me as follows: "Father: We thank the Great Spirit for what you have spoken to us and hope he will always keep your heart in this good work.

"Father: We believe there is a Great Spirit above who made all things, has made the whites as well as the Indians, and we believe there is something good after death; and we believe what you say, that the Great Spirit knows all we do.

"Father: We are astonished at you whites that when Jesus Christ was among you doing good that you white people did not pay attention to him, and believe him, and that you put him to death.

"Father: We Indians did not do this. The Great Spirit has given white people their ways to serve him and to get your living, and he has given Indians their ways to serve him and to get their living by hunting the game he gives to us.

"Father: You and your people know that the whites are getting our lands from us for almost nothing. If such good people as you and your society had advised us Indians, we and our forefathers would not have been cheated by the white people who have taken our hunting-grounds.

"Father: You do not come with maps under your arms that we have found deceit in. You come a father to advise us for our good, and not to cheat us out of our lands."

He then took strings of wampum in his hand and continued:

"Father: You and your society know that when learning was given to the Indians they became small in numbers, and some nations are extinct, and we do not know what has become of them. Our brothers, the Mohawks and the Oneidas, they were driven away from their lands.

"Father: We think learning would do us no good. We are astonished that you white people who have the good book, the Bible, and can read it and can understand it, that they are so bad and do many wicked things.

"Father: We (pointing to Farmer's Brother) cannot see that learning would do our people any good. We will leave it to those who come after us to judge for themselves. If learning was given to us, cheating would creep in among us and we would share the fate of our brothers, the Mohawks and the Oneidas, and we would not know where to go."

He then presented me with seven strings of wampum, saying:

"We want you to give these to the good society that sent you here."

We, the undersigned, were the interpreters of the above speech of Red Jacket, and assisted in committing it to writing. We hereby certify that it is as near to the ideas and phraseology expressed by him as we can write it.

Signed: William Johnston.
Nicholas Cusoc.

BUFFALOE CREEK, October 25, 1800.

ELKANAH HOLMES.

APPENDIX.

From the New York Missionary Magazine of December, 1800.

SPEECH OF FARMER'S BROTHER.

The following speech was made to me on the 21st day of October, 1800, by Farmer's Brother, Chief Sachem of the Seneca Nation, at the house of John Palmer, near the mouth of Buffaloe Creek, it being the third public talk I had with them.

ELKANAH HOLMES.

"Father: We thank the Great Spirit for allowing us to meet together this day. We have something more to say to you. When we heard your good talk we had no time to speak all we wanted to say to you.

"Father: We will now talk to you and to your good society.

"Father: The United States and the Quakers wanted some of our boys sent to them to get learning.

"Father: I gave the United States one of my grandsons to get learning.

"Father: We hoped when he got learning he would be of some good to our nation—to tell us of the good ways of the white people. Two years after he went to Philadelphia I went there on business for our nation. When there I saw my grandson, and was sorry when I saw him. He was in a tavern with some bad people—men and women—and he a boy yet. Then my thoughts that he would be of service to our nation was gone. We have no such things among us of boys having bad ways.

"Father: Some time ago I went to Geneseo and saw my grandson there in soldier clothes. He wanted me to give him two miles square to support him in going about the country.

"Father: By your good talk I would have your good society take one of our boys and take care of him and give him learning of good ways.

"Father: We hope the Great Spirit will have his eyes on this boy that we give up to your good society. We hope they will plant good things in him.

"Father: We now give to you these strings of wampum to take with our talk to your good society in New York that sent you to visit us."

WILLIAM JOHNSTON, } Interpreters.
Attest: NICHOLAS CUSOC,

ELKANAH HOLMES.

SKETCHES OF ALASKA.

Lincoln Street, Sitka.

SKETCHES OF ALASKA.

CHAPTER I.

SCENERY.

On the 21st day July, 1885, I was commissioned, by President Grover Cleveland, Marshal of the United States in and for the District of Alaska.

On the 8th of September following, together with the newly appointed Governor, Judge and District Attorney for the district, we embarked at Port Townsend, Wash., on the steamship *Idaho*, bound for Sitka, Alaska.

After a run of three hours across the strait of San Juan del Fuca, the ship was entering a cosy bay of the large Island of Vancouver, British Columbia, where is picturesquely situated the pleasant city of Victoria. The town has a population of twelve thousand inhabitants, and is noted for its genial climate, fine scenery, and, at that period, for its American Consul. To an American, the aspect at Victoria is decidedly colonial, unless it be its hackmen, who, evidently, were educated at Niagara Falls.

Upon reaching the wharf, the ship was boarded by a fussy old man, inquiring if the Alaska officials were on board. When intercepting us, he said he was the United States Consul; that he was 66 years old, with faculties unimpaired; that his wife was the daughter of the lamented Col. Baker, of Oregon, and that in war times he was clerk of a United States Senate committee; that President Hayes appointed him to his present position, and that he came to greet and invite us to call at the consulate. For all of which we thanked him, of course. During our stay at Victoria he was persistently officious, assuming to advise us how to conduct ourselves in order to maintain the dignity of our official position in due form. To our party he was a compound nuisance, and we were glad when rid of him. Josh Billings remarked that he had unsuccessfully struggled with the conundrum: "At what time of life is a man the biggest fool?" Had Josh been of our party he would have concluded that it was when consul at Victoria.

On leaving Victoria the ship makes the passage of the Gulf of Georgia, a body of salt water dividing the Island of Vancouver from the main shore of British Columbia. The passengers crowded the deck while the ship ran through narrow passages between ever green islets, made difficult and exciting by the rapid flowing of the tide. When passing the north point of Vancouver the open sea is encountered for a distance of thirty miles, when the ship enters the world's wonderland—the inland passage up the north Pacific coast. The Alexandria Archipelago, so named by Vancouver, comprises hundreds of islands, which, for eight hundred miles, fringe the coast of British Columbia and Alaska. Many of the islands and channels retain names given them by that intrepid navigator.

Able descriptive writers have essayed to portray the grandeur of these waters, one of whom writes: "The stillness of air, land and water in the early morning made it seem like the dawn of creation on some new paradise." Another writer says: "I could scarcely realize that I was in the same world left behind me." Another relates an incident. "I wish I could remember the beautiful words with which the Rev. Dr. Tiffany likened it to the glorious portal of future life. I do remember a gentleman standing near me remarked: 'I did not believe that God ever made anything so beautiful as this.' To which I involuntarily replied, but not irreverently, 'I did not believe that he could.'"

During my stay in Alaska much of my time was spent in traversing these channels, and my observation could not detect wherein the above descriptions were overdrawn. No pen can faithfully describe the grandeur there presented. The observer meets with many surprises—new scenery constantly appearing as the steamer pursues its winding course among the islands. Many whales are seen projecting their sable backs above the surface of water, and at near approach dive into its depths, flaunting their tails in defiance as they longitudinally disappear from view. In ludicrous contrast to the majesty of the scene, was a dude on the upper deck firing at a huge whale with No. 6 shot.

Prominent among these passages is Glenville channel. It is about forty miles long, a half-mile wide, and mostly straight as an arrow. Lined on either side by mountain walls, clothed with evergreen up to the timber line, thence is presented a region of rock, vast in extent, all of which is surmounted by a region of snow and ice—these aerial glaciers glistening in the sunlight with "more than silvery whiteness."

An approaching steamer, when in this channel, so near the mountain walls, loses the majesty it presents in open water, appearing as insignificant as a house-fly crawling on a billiard table. Occasionally, a local snow-storm can be seen dancing a Highland fling on a mountain-top, while a genial atmosphere of sixty degrees prevails on the deck of the steamer. Numerous tiny cataracts leap down hundreds of feet perpendicularly. They look, as I heard a lady remark, "like huge satin ribbons, hanging down the mountain walls." Throughout the archipelago hundreds of evergreen islets decorate the waters, "like gems on a coronet." The beholder of this sublime scenery is struck with wonder and awe at its more than earthly grandeur.

We called at Douglas Island, where there is a producing gold mine, and a large stamp-mill in full operation. It was then the property of Senator Jones, of Nevada, and other mining capitalists. The Senator was a passenger on the ship from Victoria. He is an agreeable, level-headed man of the world, enthusiastic in the future of Alaska as a gold-producing region. The Senator was accompanied by his wife, whose superior personality, and kindly greetings accorded to strangers on shipboard, is a pleasant memory.

CHAPTER II.

SITKA.

After a pleasant and interesting passage of seven days, the ship landed at Sitka, the Alaskan capital. The town is situated on the west shore of Baranoff Island, at the head of a deep bay, twenty miles from the outer capes. The capes are about fifteen miles apart, the shores of the bay approaching to within a distance of five miles at the head of the bay, where is located the town. Baranoff is an outer island of the group, its east shore being about fifty miles from the main-land. It is eighty miles long from north to south, maintaining a width of thirty miles, in latitude 57.2, and longitude 135 degrees west from Greenwich.

The town of Sitka is built on a level plateau, containing about three hundred acres, fifteen feet above high tide. This area is washed on two sides by the waters of the bay, and otherwise walled in by high mountains, whose snow region is three thousand feet above the tide. Fronting the town, one thousand feet distant, are a cordon of islands across the bay, clothed with evergreen, the channels between affording ample entrance to a commodious harbor, thus forming a cosy amphitheatre, where nestles the quaint little town of hewn logs and whitewashed walls. With its primitive architecture, its grassy courts and graveled walks, its waters and islets, its traders and their shops, its Indians and their canoes, Sitka is much like the old town of Mackinaw, at the head of Lake Huron.

Included in the population of Sitka, at that period, were about one hundred Russian Creoles, quiet and industrious people. Of Americans proper there were about a like number, including civil officials, naval officers and their families. The adjoining Indian village, or "ranche," as they're called, contained about one thousand natives, men, women and children. At the front, facing the waters of the bay, is an open space of about three acres, called "The Green," appropriately so, as the grass thereon remains fresh and green throughout the year. Here are mounted two Dahlgren guns, with a number of ancient Russian cannon keeping them company, altogether an imposing battery to repel a fleet of canoes. The Government buildings face the Green, and, like the old cannon, are relics of the Russian nobles, who in days of yore held high carnival at Sitka.

Out seaward, on the north shore of the bay, stands majestic Mt. Edgecomb, a subdued volcano. When Captain Cook was there in 1796, it was in an angry mood, belching out smoke, cinders, fire and brimstone, but now it is an orderly and conservative volcano.

There is a large mission establishment at Sitka, including an Industrial School, where little Indians are taught to read and write, the boys blacksmithing, shoe-making and carpenter work, and the girls to cook, sew and knit. The day following our arrival the newly arrived Governor and Marshal were invited to dine at the mission. When standing in line awaiting introduction to the ladies there resident, the hostess advanced and offered her hand to the Marshal, saying: "You are very welcome to Sitka, Governor." Her greeting was cordially reciprocated, when she was advised of her mistaken identity, and assured that it was quite justified when contrasting our personal appearance. The incident gave zest to our introductions, and hastened our acquaintance with the people there assembled, and caused the constant watching of the Governor for an opportunity to get even, until he succeeded in so doing. We were shown through the work-shops, where I noticed a ten-year-old boy, with freckled face and sandy hair. The novelty of a red-haired Indian prompted the inquiry, "What's your name?" Promptly came the answer, "Mike Murphy." Eureka! An Irish Indian! Who'd a thunk it?

Shortly after our arrival occurred an incident novel and interesting to a "tenderfoot." A native holding a coil of line, waded out from the beach and hove its hook end far out into the water, and then returned to shore. He soon began to haul in, hand over hand, and soon with greater exertion, as if he had a bite from something having at least two rows of teeth; and sure enough, for there appeared in the surf a lusty halibut, making the water boil by the handy wielding of his tail. Mr. Indian again waded out and gave the fish a smart rap on the head with a club, and then, aided by a helper, dragged his captive to the beach amid the applause of Governor, Marshal, squaws, mugwumps and hoodlums.

In Sitka bear-skins are a legal tender, and a house hold article in all well-regulated families. No sleeping room is complete without a bear-skin spread in front of the bed to receive your feet when in a bare state. Their market price was $5.00 each. Governor Swineford paid an octogenarian squaw $6.00 for one. When asked why the extra dollar was demanded, she coolly replied, "Big Chief pay much."

Sitka is a naval station, and a vessel of war is stationed there, with its company of marines quartered on shore, where they beat and blow "taps," early and late, and drill on the Green.

In Sitka there is an old Greek Church, with a tower containing a chime of six bells, which supply the town with music galore. There, also, is a colony of ravens, the identical "ominous birds of yore," occupying an adjacent mountain-side. They make daily visits, and hold dress parade on the Green. Their gyrations are in fair imitation of the marines in their morning drill; the birds coming immediately after. Seals and sea-lions sun themselves on the outer rocks, while the festive dolphin and porpoise perform their gymnastic exercises within the inner bay. The weather clerk flew his scientific kites from the top of the "Castle," the most pretentious structure made by human hands in all Alaska.

THE GREEK CHURCH.

The most interesting relic of the Russian era in Alaska is the Russo-Greek Church of St. Michael at Sitka. It is designed and constructed in the form of a Greek cross, like similar edifices in the mother country, and is the only one of similar construction on the western continent. It is prominently situated, facing the sea at the head of the street running up from the landing. The front entrance is through the square base of the tower, in the second story of which is the chime of bells. From the tower rises a tall, symmetrical spire, topped by a golden cross, comprising four distinct crosses. Back of the tower, surmounting the main portion of the structure, is a massive metal covered oriental dome. From the cupola above the dome, rises a spire, supporting a large golden ball, and above the ball is a compound Greek cross nine feet high. The church was erected ninety years ago, and now, while its exterior is an old, weather-worn concern, the interior has its original presentment of an oriental paradise. One wing is used as a chapel, and therein, beside a unique font, is a large painting of the Virgin and Child, a counterpart of the celebrated painting at Moscow. All the drapery is of silver and the halo of gold. The chancel is elevated, and approached by three broad steps up to two golden bronzed doors, ornamented by solid silver images of the patron saints. All the panels are decorated by fine oil paintings, which good judges say must have been executed by a master hand. Above the chancel is a painting of the Last Supper, covered, like the Madonna, with silver, as are two others, one each side of the altar. Across the threshold of these doors no woman is allowed to step, and through the inner one none but the priest and his superiors are allowed to enter. The walls are hung with portraits in oil, and the general effect is rich in the extreme. The bishop's crown is covered with pearls and amethysts. The floors are strewn with rich oriental rugs, and around stand huge candelabra of solid silver, bearing colored waxen candles six inches in diameter and six feet high. The incongruity of such splendor in a remote wilderness is not the least considered among the curious things connected with this strange edifice.

From the tower of the church the mountain scenery is extremely picturesque. A notable scene is Cross Mountain. Near its towering summit is a perpetual glacier, which in form is a perfect imitation of the Holy Cross, symmetrically real to the view. Probably no other body of ice is as reverentially considered as is the glacier on Cross Mountain.

The adherents of the Greek Church at Sitka have a unique annual ceremony. Headed by their priest, who is flanked on either side by men bearing a large, open book, from which he reads in a loud voice, they march in procession about the town, to "drive the devil out" from all places in which he may have become installed during the year past. This ceremony has an air of solemnity about it that commands the respectful attention of spectators. To an American it presents a scene decidedly quaint and foreign.

Governor A. P. Swineford was a citizen of Marquette, Mich., where, as legislator, mayor, and editor of the *Mining Journal*, he had developed sufficient gall to become a territorial governor. While *en route* to his dominion he conceived the audacity of introducing a printer's outfit into the peaceful solitude of Alaska. At Portland, Oregon, the conspiracy was promoted by his purchase of a hand press and other material to print a newspaper, which was shipped to Sitka, where, for a time, the disturbing element was closely confined.

The official labors of the Alaskan executive are not to a great degree exhaustive, consisting, chiefly, in conversing emotionally with the natives (making motions to Indians), gathering curios and looking for his interpreter. Therefore Governor Swineford had abundant leisure to indulge his propensity to print and edit a newspaper without interfering with his official labors.

At a meeting of citizens and officials, a publication company was formed with a paid-up capital of six hundred dollars—the cost of the printing outfit—and it was then resolved to publish a newspaper at Sitka. In the person of the Governor the association had available a practical publisher, printer and editor, whose reputation justified the belief that their contemplated newspaper would be published in form, and edited, if need be, with audacity. With the aid of a typo discovered among the marines, the Governor set up the press in a vacant Russian hut, and in due time appeared a full-fledged newspaper—*The Alaskan.*

Most new enterprises boast of a specialty, and that of *The Alaskan* was of being the most westerly, most northerly and most remote publication on the American continent. Three of its four pages were filled with solid matter, descriptive of Alaska, its climate, resources and needs in the way of congressional legislation, written by the master hand of the Governor. The remaining columns were diversely illumined with local paragraphs contributed by a minor official, whose service in that direction was demanded by the managing editor, notwithstanding his genius had never been thus directed—"which will make the newspaper interesting," said the Governor.

Following are sample locals in the initial number of *The Alaskan:*

To a Sitkan the pleasures of life are blended with uncertainty as to the struggle between a monthly mail and the deep sea. All else is serene.

A charitable lady placed on our desk a dish filled with cookies. Early in our career we learned to admire the toothsome concrete, and the good lady has our thanks. Later—While momentarily absent, the managing editor clandestinely entered our sanctum and cooked them all. The next mail will bring newspapers dated to November first, all antedating the elections now decided. A cold-potato diet is the reading of campaign literature after election is past. But we antipodes must endure the affliction as we do our old debts—with Christian resignation.

A custom of Alaska Indians, incident to their superstition, is that of not removing their dead out the doorway of a house, but through the smokehole in the roof, in order, perhaps, to make a scoop on the evil spirit. Calls for the service of this tenderfoot as pall-bearer on such occasions are declined in advance. The spectacle of we, us, leading a funeral procession down the roof of a house must ever be lost to science.

It is recorded that this is the season of the greatest rainfall at Sitka. But the present feature is alternate rain and sunshine, and unless one of the contestants weakens, there will be a dead heat for first money. Such is the force of habit, even on a strong mind. Though we sold our trotter before starting for Alaska, our pen, unless under a strong pull, will break and perpetrate a turf item. However, this being a weather item, the digression may escape the scrutiny of the managing editor, and as well as any answer his call for copy. If not, why not?

Such commodity did the Governor of Alaska consider "made a newspaper interesting."

A favorite prerogative of Alaska's executive is to coddle the Indians, to preside at their pow-wows and referee their domestic troubles, which duties Governor Swineford discharged with infinite zest. A native of Mormon proclivities, whose dual wives had prosecuted a scratch-fight, appeared with the combatants before the executive tribunal to have the matter adjudicated. Whereupon the Governor promulgated a code of divorce—arbitrarily separated the untutored native from his best-looking wife. The decree was respected for a time, but finally the women became reconciled and again the trio appeared at court, praying that the divorced wife be restored to her former marital relations. The court explained how this "couldn't be done," and lectured the applicants on the enormity of a good Indian having two wives. And then, with Solomonic wisdom, decided that the husband could choose between the two which he would take for his wife, and that must settle the matter for all time. That was a "decision as was a decision," one with decided effect, creating a lively conflict between the women, from which the court made good escape, taking refuge in a convenient billiard saloon. The case went over the term.

On another occasion the Governor displayed wise judicial function. A vagabond Indian doctor had imposed his legerdemain upon an invalid sexagenarian squaw, until his fees had exacted her last blanket. The patient, not convalescent, applied to the executive for redress. The complainant was attended by two stalwart natives, who were by the court invested with official authority—tying a ribbon, taken from a bunch of cigars, around the wrist of each—and ordering them to arrest and bring the offender into court forthwith. The royal insignia of an Indian doctor is a superfluity of hair, in the manner of a foot-ball lunatic, the massive quantity of which supplies his healing power, and by which he set much store. With the offender, and about a dozen blankets in evidence, the court opened, and after a decree restoring the blankets to their proper owner, practical punishment was inflicted upon the culprit, the court barber shaving his head as hair less as a billiard ball. After the shave a coat of red paint was applied to his scalp, after which the court kicked him out of his office, as fine a looking fellow as ever broke open a smoke-house.

On the arrival of the civil officials in Alaska, the commander of the naval vessel stationed there denied social recognition to the plebeian representatives of the Government, removing his vessel to Juneau in contempt of their presence at Sitka, a proceeding privately condemned by other officers of the ship. In his report to the department, the lieutenant-commander, as reported in the *Army and*

Navy Journal, gave as the reason of such removal: "In order to secure a better harbor during an anticipated equinoctial storm," a reason absurd, owing to the fact that Sitka harbor is exceptionally secure, while that of Juneau is to a degree insecure.

In recognition of the courteous treatment accorded them by the naval officer, writers on *The Alaskan* kept him stirred up with compliments in the way of pointed paragraphs pertinent to his quibbling. Specimens thereof are here appended:

> Fears are entertained for the safety of the equinoctial storm, now overdue. The arrival of the Army and Navy Journal is anxiously awaited. It may have tidings from it.

> Hoop-e-la! The mail steamer is due! There's going to be a wedding, and the gunboat is safe at Juneau! Arise and sing!

> > "An anchorage I've found,
> > Where's good holding ground,
> > To dwell I'm determined
> > At this mining town."

Such was *The Alaskan* in 1885-86. A copy of the initial number was sent to all prominent journals in the country, and the complimentary notices it received were greater in number and emphasis than ever before accorded to a country newspaper—the New York *Herald* devoting a column to quotations therefrom.

CHAPTER III.

GOVERNMENT BUILDINGS.

The historic structures at Sitka, known as the Government Buildings, consisted of Baranoff Castle, recently destroyed by fire, the Barracks, so called by the Russians, and the Customs House. These buildings are massive, and of much solidity in their construction. The outer walls and hall partitions are of timbers twenty-four inches square throughout, other timbers, joists and posts are twelve inches square. When laid, each wall timber had its top hollowed to receive the rounded bottom of its rider. Before receiving its rider, each timber was secured in its place by copper bolts, one and one-half inches in diameter, driven through into the second lower one. These buildings were intended to be earthquake-proof, their predecessors having been tumbled down by such disturbances in 1827.

The Barracks in size is eighty by ninety feet on the ground, and three stories high, each story divided by a hall ten feet in width. The outer walls are covered with siding painted a dingy yellow. This building was the military headquarters of the Russians, but Uncle Sam has accorded to it a more peaceable existence. The lower story is the territorial prison. In the second story are the offices of the civil officials and their sleeping apartments, rent free. The upper story is devoted to the court rooms of the United States District Court.

The reason these buildings were bolted with copper, when iron would have answered as well, was explained by an old resident of Sitka. When the Russians were trading with the Sandwich Islands from Sitka, there was a shipyard at the latter place where many vessels were built. When the buildings were commenced, the work was delayed by the non-arrival of the vessel from Russia having on board the iron for the new buildings. Baranoff, learning that the vessel had been wrecked, ordered work on the buildings to proceed, using a quantity of copper bolts then on hand at the ship-yard. Some of the timbers next to the ground have decayed, where the copper bolts are plainly visible.

Like the island on which it stood, the Castle took its name from the Russian Governor Baranoff, who was educated a tyrant in the Siberian school of horrors, and his reign at Sitka attested the high grade of that institution. There he ruled "with a tyranny that began with the knout, and ended with the axe."

Prior to the advent of Baranoff, two attempts to found a settlement on the island were made by the Russians under protection of the Archangel Gabriel, but in both cases, the protection failed to protect the colony from massacre by the natives.

In 1801 Baranoff came, bringing guns and gun powder, to which the Indians paid more deference than to the Muscovite religion. Baranoff rebuilt and fortified the town. A line of stockade and two block houses of his fortification are still in evidence at Sitka. The famous Baranoff

GOVERNMENT BUILDINGS.

Castle, recently burned, was constructed similar to the Barracks, in size 75 by 125, with two stories and dome. It was situated on a rocky eminence, rising sixty feet perpendicular from the level, having a top surface of about one-fourth of an acre in extent. Baranoff fortified the elevation with batteries of cannon—the historic guns being still at Sitka—the property of Uncle Sam.

An interesting sketch of history concerning the Castle, is given by Mrs. General Collis, of which the following is an extract:

> "It will be difficult to work the imagination up to the point of believing that this now desolate old place was once the home of nobility—the scene of festivities, given with imperial sanction and ceremony, but such is the fact. Here princes and princesses of the blood royal have eaten their caviare, quaffed their vodhka, and measured a minuet, surrounded by a court, fresh from the palaces of Moscow and St. Petersburg. It was in this very house that Lady Franklin spent several weeks of her aged life in the hope that she might find some trace—dead or alive—of her adventurous husband, Sir John. It was here that Secretary Seward resided for a time, when on his trip to see with his own eyes the vast territory peacefully acquired for his country, by the sagacity of himself and Senator Sumner, at a cost of two cents per acre."

Until recently, the martial force of Alaska was wholly naval. One vessel is stationed at Sitka, where she is idle nine months of the year. In summer a tour of the archipelago is usually made. A naval store house is established at Sitka, and other naval vessels are frequent in the harbor. Some of the officers have their families at Sitka, housed on shore, their assignment to that station meaning three years absence from a distant home. They are pleasant and joyous people, who, together with the civil officials and their families, constitute a social community cemented with a sympathy born of mutual deprivation of the society of relatives and friends while resident on that distant evergreen shore. Life at Sitka is usually agreeable, the climate is genial, the surroundings novel and picturesque, living facilities are good, and with more frequent communication with the inside world. Sitka would be far from an undesirable place for residence.

NATIVE INDIANS.

Adjoining the town of Sitka on the north is the Indian Ranch, containing about seven or eight hundred swarthy natives. The Indians of Southeastern Alaska are a race distinct from those of the Western tribes in America. Their race name is Klingets. Their outward characteristic are coarse hair, black and straight, large black eyes, thick lips and flat faces; generally of medium stature, and well-developed chests, arms and shoulders, while their lower limbs are shrunken and crooked. Much of their life is spent in their canoes, squatting on their feet and ankles for a seat, hence their deformity, while their constant paddling develops their breast, arms and shoulders. They have no tribal relations, but flock in families, so called, on separate islands, which they claim as their exclusive domain. The members of each family, the Sitkans for instance, assume blood relationship; all are parents uncles, cousins and aunts, and they do not intermarry. When a man wants a wife he goes to another island and buys one, paying therefor an agreed number of blankets, which, with them, are a legal tender to the amount of two silver dollars. If the suitor is rejected, his lacerated affections are soothed to a normal state by a payment of blankets to him. His enterprise fails not of reward—either a wife or a bundle of blankets. When compelled to take gold coin in trade, they go directly to a trader and get it changed to silver. They detect spurious silver readily, but are suspicious of gold, nursing a legend that long ago a trading vessel visited the islands and imposed upon their ancestors a quantity of spurious gold coin.

Unlike other Indians, the men perform the drudgery. The women are the bosses and untie the purse-strings. Nothing is bought or sold without their consent. With them this system has the best results, as it undoubtedly would have in many civilized communities. They are sharp traders, getting more for what they sell and paying less for what they buy, whisky excepted, than any other people I ever heard of. Put a score or more of them into Chatham street and within a few years they would own the street.

The Klingets obtain their subsistence mostly from the sea. They eat the flesh of animals but sparingly. All kinds of fish and other sea life are their main food supplies. They have two annual festivals—the salmon and the berry festivals. These are celebrated by a procession of canoes decorated with green twigs and small flags daubed with images of the raven, fish, bear and other animals. The salmon festival is for the liberal run of salmon, and the berry festival for the abundant yield of wild berries the season brought forth. A long procession of canoes filled with dusky natives, who paddle about the harbor singing a wild refrain the live-long day, with a feast and carousal at night, are the salmon and berry festivals at Sitka.

Among the wild berries of Alaska, the salmon berry, so called from its vermilion color, like the meat of a salmon, is pre-eminent. Conical in shape, and, when ripe, the size of a large horse-chestnut, they are in appearance inviting and of delicious flavor. When leaving the country a keen regret was the parting with the salmon berry.

NATIVE HANDIWORK.

The canoes paddled over Alaskan waters are complete dug-outs, from what must have been, in some cases, monarchs of the forest. Their shells range from one to three inches in thickness, and in length they range from nine to seventy feet, and with proportionate width and depth. A war canoe at Sitka is sixty feet in length, six feet in width, and twenty-eight inches deep, with a projecting prow at either end, five feet long. Its bottom and sides, inboard and outboard, are as smooth as planed marble, and in its entire length does not present a flaw. The model of this mammoth canoe is as symmetrical as a pleasure yacht in waters of civilization. The natives navigate their canoes expertly, wielding paddles as dexterously as a cowboy manages a mustang.

The Klingets are a festive race, paying much attention to their amusements—potlaching, dancing, gambling and canoe-racing—and have a keen relish for the fantastic. The stock of masks of a family are numbered by hundreds, presenting faces old, young, weird and horrid—mostly horrid—and all of home manufacture. Seemingly, by nature, they are endowed with a faculty for carving on wood, stone, slate, and on the softer metals. Their work in silver—rings, bracelets and like trinkets, which they sell to the whites—is of extraordinary merit. Their working tool for carving is usually an old jack-knife, ground to a point. They carve images of animals and birds, from which is assumed their respective families sprung—the bear, the raven, and so on. Sculptured totem poles, some of which are thirty feet high, stand in their ranches, to which they pay homage. They daub images on their canoes, paddles and masks with a brush made of goat hair, and obtain colors from the juices of roots. The basket work of the women is superior to a great degree, some of which is so firmly constructed as to hold water. Their horn spoons are a superior article. They take the horn of the mountain goat, saw it lengthwise, and soak in hot water until pliable, then press on a wooden model into spoon shape, and then the handles are carved with surprising excellence. With the spoons they feast out of bowls made of horn or wood, elaborately carved. The Chilkat blankets, made by the family of that name in former times, but now a lost art, probably, are the most unique article of savage manufacture. They are woven from the long hair of the mountain sheep and goat, and are used for decoration when dancing and masquerading. They are in color a combination of black, white, blue and yellow, and figured emblematical of family genealogy and heraldry. They are held as heirlooms by the more opulent families, and at times are sold to tourists for from one hundred to three hundred dollars each, according to their condition and quality of make.

SUPERSTITIONS.

When an Alaska Indian dies in a house, his body is not taken out through the doorway, but out the smoke-hole in the roof. This in order—to borrow a journalistic phrase—to make a scoop on the evil spirit. When charged with witchcraft, they cremate the body of the dead. I witnessed the ceremonies on such an occasion at Sitka. First, I inspected the crematory. It was a crib structure of green balsam logs, in size about six feet long, two feet wide and five feet deep, half filled with dry kindlings, saturated with coal oil. When entering the house I saw the corpse sitting bolt upright in a corner, on the floor, and from feet to armpits sewed up in a dirty blanket, leaving head, shoulders and arms bare. It was a withered, dried-up old man, weighing about seventy pounds. He looked like a witch, and I half believe he had been one—at least I justified the supposition. A mourner raised the body and poked it through the smoke-hole, and another, on the roof, seized it and carried it down and dumped it into the crib. With the deceased was deposited his personal property, consisting of an ancient shot-gun, a butcher knife, a couple of blankets, and sundry trinkets. Then the crib was filled up and covered with dry wood, when more coal oil was poured on and the thing set on fire. Then a dozen of the mourners joined hands and circled around the burning-pile, howling doleful lamentations, joined by a chorus of wolf dogs in concert, until the fire burned out. Then they put the roasted carcass into a wooden box about three feet square, having a gable roof, placing it with a congregation of the like in their cemetery, above ground. They looked like a village of dog-houses.

The original traders to the Pacific coast came in ships from Boston, hence all whites are called "Boston men" by the natives. When a mining company imported Mexican burros for packing to the mine, in deference to their elongated ears the natives called them "Boston rabbits."

COMPENSATION.

When employed by or in company of whites, an Indian is killed or injured, his family demand compensation therefor, either in money or blankets. At Sitka an Indian in jail stabbed himself to death with a pair of pointed scissors, snatched from a fellow-prisoner, who was mending his clothing. A hundred or more Indians then proceeded to the Marshal's office and demanded three hundred blankets for the death of their brother.

A miner employed a native to pack some drills to his claim, and before starting gave him a drink of whisky from a bottle taken from a cupboard. The Indian's squaw entered the door in time to see the bottle replaced, and she subsequently returned, broke into the cabin, and drank two bottles of the miner's whisky. The next day she was found dead on the floor of the cabin. Her family demanded one hundred blankets of the miner, which he paid, in order to exempt himself from a parlous state. The barbarous demand of an eye for an eye and a tooth for a tooth is their creed, and, unless pacified, someone may be found dead—a life taken in compensation; be he guilty or innocent, there is no distinction in that respect.

No sense of gratitude abides with these natives, other than a seeming acknowledgment of the beneficence of the Great Spirit, evinced in their salmon and berry festivals. A fishing schooner was scudding before a furious gale of wind out at sea, when two Indians in a canoe were espied, who had been blown off the coast. The Indians were rescued, but owing to the severity of the tempest their canoe was lost. The master of the schooner landed the rescued men at their village, where a demand for pay for the lost canoe was made, joined by the men whose lives he had saved. Apparently a heart is not included in their anatomy, but in lieu thereof they have a gizzard.

When aged sixteen the children in the Industrial School usually return to the ranches, but exist differently. They eat off tables and crockery, use knives and forks, sit on chairs, wear store clothes, play poker, and whip their wives, like other half-civilized people.

CHAPTER IV.
JUNEAU.

The American-built town of Alaska is Juneau, named for Joseph Juneau, a descendant of the Mackinaw, Green Bay and Milwaukee family of that name, who, in 1880, first discovered its adjacent gold deposits. The town is situated on Gasteneau Channel, a passage of deep salt water nearly a mile wide, dividing Douglas Island from the main shore. By the channels among and around islands Juneau is about one hundred and eighty miles northeast of Sitka. Together with Douglas City and the extensive gold mine on the island opposite—virtually one community—there now is a population of about five thousand. The town is located at the mouth of Gold Creek, a small stream tumbling down a gorge between mountains 3,000 feet high, which wall the town on three sides, where it is picturesquely nestled. Following up a winding and ascending gulch for three miles, you come to Silver Bow Basin, a large area encircled by mountain-tops. Here are the famous placer diggings, where many thousands of dollars of gold-dust and nuggets have been gathered by the sturdy miners who founded and built up Juneau.

The miners and traders of Juneau are of the better class of American pioneers, who in early manhood left their homes to march over the plains and mountains to the Pacific Slope, and there grew up with the sage brush, and since have prospected the gravel beds of the mountain streams from Mexico to Alaska, men whose general characteristics are generosity, fidelity and honor, and who live in full confidence of the integrity of each other. Should one prove unfaithful, his case is duly considered, and, when adjudged guilty, he is warned to leave the country, and, for prudential reasons, such warnings are promptly obeyed.

CLIMATE AND VEGETATION.

The climate of Alaska is as varied as that of the country extending from Hudson Bay to the Gulf of Mexico. The Pacific Coast and the Aleutian Islands receive the warm breath of the Japan current, providing those portions with a winter climate of the temperature of the States of Maryland and Tennessee. The island of Attou, an American, lying in the waters of the Eastern Hemisphere, has a climate as genial as that of Italy. The annual rain-fall on Southern Alaska is eighty inches, about double that of the Middle States. Usually it is a continuous drizzle for a week or more, facetiously called a dry rain, as clothes hung under a shed will dry during a down-pour. Shoes do not mould nor clothing become musty in the dampest weather. Up north, in the valley of the Yukon, where frost penetrates the earth twenty feet, the mercury often marks ninety degrees in July and August. About seventy-two is as high as I experienced while four years in Alaska, and never at zero.

Alaska is not a grain country. The cereals run to stalks, and do not head and ripen—too much rain and not sufficient sunshine. Garden truck grows luxuriantly and yields abundantly. Many species of wild berries ripen in great abundance.

FISHES, FURS, FORESTS AND ANIMALS.

Practically, to an unlimited extent, food fishes abound in Alaskan waters. Cod, salmon, mackerel, halibut and herring, the chief fishes of commerce, are more abundant than in other waters of the globe. When aboard ship, and passing out of a narrow entrance to a bay, where emptied a mountain stream, the captain told me to look over forward and see the fish. The ship was plowing through a run of salmon, casting them out of the water from either side of the stem. So eager were the salmon to reach fresh water, that the narrow entrance to the bay was massed with fish.

In Alaska furs are a staple commodity. The value of the pelts annually secured is counted by millions. Sea and land otter, seal and sea-lion, sable-martin, beaver, and the several species of fox, are the most valuable. The most precious of furs is the sea-otter, and Alaskan waters supply the majority of pelts marketed. For a prime one its captor receives $150, and Russian nobility are his best customers. Next in value are the black, blue, white and silver fox, the most valuable bringing from thirty to one hundred dollars for green pelts. A group of islands, called Fox Islands, abound with foxes. An enterprising hunter leased a smaller one from Uncle Sam, and has it stocked with these rare animals, which he feeds and domesticates. Only the males are killed. A fortune awaits the foxy genius who has established a fox-farm under the shadow of the Arctic Circle. Alaska is the sportsman's paradise. Myriads of wild fowl darken the waters of channels, inlets, bays and rivers. Mountain-sides are alive with grouse. The black and brown bear are plentiful—the white species adheres to the frozen region. The brown and black bear are expert fishermen. When salmon invest the mountain streams bruin wades in, and with his paw deftly lands them, and then his bearship banquets on fresh salmon.

CHAPTER V.

MINES AND MINERALS.

Almost every known mineral is found in Alaska. Gold, silver, copper, mica, iron, coal, marble and slate are most common. Coal is abundant, cropping out in many sections. At Cook's Inlet the crew of the U. S. Cutter *Corwin* took from a bank facing the water seventy tons of cannel coal to the vessel in small boats within eighteen hours. Their mining tools were crowbars. The engineer of the cutter stated that the coal was high grade for steam purposes.

On Douglas Island is the largest producing gold mine and plant in the world—an enlarged out-cropping, 2,000 feet long, 600 feet wide and of unknown depth; an elevated ridge of free milling decomposed quartz, with the largest stamp-mill in the world at its base. The mill has forty-eight batteries, with five head of stamps to each battery—in all 240 stamps—all under one roof, all pounding at once, and all operated by single power. The mineral is reduced to gold bullion at a cost of less than one dollar per ton of rock. The mill crushes 600 tons of rock each twenty-four hours. The rock averages four dollars per ton, gold. The mine and mill are situated within 200 yards of deep-water navigation to all seaports. In Alaska there are other producing mines, but none, as yet, as extensive as the wonderful mine on Douglas Island.

Placer mining is extensively prosecuted on the Yukon and its branches and in the vicinity of Juneau. The annual increase of production is large. This often characterized barren and frozen region is the only unorganized territory Uncle Sam ever possessed that paid a net revenue. Its original cost has been returned to the treasury by the seal fisheries alone. The annual output of its mines and fisheries for the past three years has been $6,000,000. So says the Interior Department. The greater development to come, probably, will not be over-estimated.

YUKON RIVER.

The majestic Yukon rises somewhere in the unexplored region of British America, entering Alaska near the fifty-ninth parallel, thence it courses north westerly to the Arctic Circle; thence southwesterly to the Behring Sea. Steamboats drawing four feet of water ascend the river 2,000 miles from its mouth. Some of its numerous branches are alike navigable for 300 miles. When flowing southwest in Alaska its usual width is about five miles, interspersed with numerous islands. It empties into the sea through four separate channels, having a distance of 100 miles across its mouths and deltas. In the interior at times it widens to twenty miles, forming a chain of lakes navigable throughout their area. The mountain portions of the Yukon and its branches abound in precious metals, and that remote region is at the present writing the objective point of many adventurous spirits seeking the yellow metal.

The above account of the Yukon was written in 1889, and now, that gold in abundant quantities has been found in the region, the world will soon know more of that distant and resourceful country.

When at Juneau in October, 1886, a party of thirty miners arrived there fresh from the Yukon country, coming out over the Chilcoot trail, headed by the brothers Dinsmore, of California. They went in by the same route the previous month of March. At the time, a monthly steamer was the only conveyance out of Alaska to civilization, and which the miners missed by three days. Then they went to the supply store of W. F. Reed, a well-known old miner, to deposit their gold, which, in deer-skin bags, they unrolled from their packs of blankets. Reed removed from his safe books and shelves and then proceeded to stow therein the weighty little sacks, in the manner of placing brick in a cart. When all were stowed the door refused to close sufficient to be locked, but Reed vigorously flung his number eleven boot against the bags for a time, and finally succeeded in locking the safe door. The party had about $33,000, obtained from the gravel beds of Lewis River, a branch of the Yukon.

VOLCANOES AND GLACIERS.

In 1887 naval officers reported officially that there were then seven active volcanoes on the Aleutian Islands. Recent reports represent a more general awakening of these subterranean fires, there now being more than twenty of heretofore extinct craters, belching out fire and cinders. The show of such force now in action in Alaska is the greatest known to the continent. Bogaslow, and an adjacent island, recently separated by two miles of deep water, are now one island. The newly appearing *terra firma* is as smooth and black as if just from a molten state. Of the majestic scenery of Alaska, these burning mountains are an important portion.

Our pen is unable to fully describe the grandeur of the huge glaciers that come down to the sea from the mountains of Alaska. Prof. John Muir, the explorer of the glacier named for him, gives its face dimensions thus:

> The front is about three miles wide. The height of the wall of ice is about three hundred feet, but soundings show that seven hundred feet of the glacier is under water, while still a third portion is buried in moraine material. Were the water and rocky *detritus* away, a wall of solid ice would be presented more than one thousand feet high. Five miles back of its face the ice is ten miles wide. This one glacier contains more ice than the 1,100 glaciers of the Alps combined.

When considered that this world of ice is crowded down to the sea between mountain walls forty feet per day, human imagination may estimate the volume of rumble and roar attendant upon its tumble from a height into the sea. Imagine a huge iceberg of the bulk of the Ellicott Square building—many are larger—tumbling from a height into deep water. When on ship-board, anchored two miles away, on such an occasion, the first to come is a tremendous crash, followed, as Prof. Muir faithfully describes, by a deep, deliberate, long drawn out, thundering roar. Then rolling comes a monster wave, causing the ship to roll as if struggling with the like in an ocean tempest.

The Muir glacier comes down to the sea from a range of lofty mountains, where stand in line the three majesties, Mt. Crillon, Mt. Fairweather and Mt. La Perouse, the lowest of which penetrates 15,000 feet skyward.

Taku glacier, occasionally witnessed by tourists, is as high as the Muir, but not more than a mile wide. In the sunlight, when from its face is reflected the varied and radiant colors of the rainbow, it is magnificently beautiful to behold.

The mammoth glacier that comes down to the sea from Mount St. Elias, presents on its front a wall of blue-tinged ice four hundred feet high and thirty miles wide. The ice falling from this monster into the sea would duplicate the glaciers of Switzerland each month in the year. The thundering sounds made by icebergs, falling daily from this huge glacier, would drown the roars of Niagara made in a thousand years.

In ancient times the great wonders of the world were attributed to the work of human hands, among which were the Pyramids of Egypt and the Colossus of Rhodes. Could the sages who conferred such distinction witness the movement of an Alaskan glacier, methinks a revision of judgment would transfer such honors to Nature's wonders in the New World. The Muir glacier alone has greater majesty than the mooted seven wonders of the world of ancient times—more than all the creation of human hands combined.

Yet Americans flock to Europe and climb the rugged steeps of the Alps to look upon wonderful glaciers. They gaze with amazement upon the majesty of Mt. Blanc, the only European peer of an Alaskan mountain. They traverse the Old World seeking natural scenery of a grandeur incomparable to that left behind at home, and by them unseen. The great European mountain is not of surpassing interest, and once a Yankee told him so:

> "How-de-do, Mt. Blanc? I vow I'm glad to meet ye!
> A thundering grist of miles I've come to greet ye.
> I'm from America, where we've got a fountain—
> Niagara it is called—where you might lave
> Your mighty phiz; then you could shirt and shave

In old Kentuck—in our Mammoth Cave;
Or take a snooze, when in want of rest,
On our big prairies—away out West;
Or when you're dry, might cool your heated liver,
In sipping up our Mississippi River.
Come over, Blanc—don't make the least ado,
Bring Switzerland with you—and the Swiss girls, too!"

During the past decade Alaskan scenery has been witnessed by naturalists from many lands, all of whom proclaim wonder and astonishment at its magnificent grandeur. Through the summer months twilight remains to the exclusion of darkness, when the enchanted traveler, foregoing the pleasures of sleep, remains on the deck of the ship, there to inhale the blended fragrance of air, land and water, to look upon the ever green isles and islets as the passing ship glides o'er the surface of the placid waters, to gaze upon the recurring wonders of Nature, to view the wild emotions and the flowing of the tide. Such is Alaska—our Land of the Midnight Sun!

THE FORESTER.

LINES SUGGESTED BY A VISIT TO A LONELY DWELLER IN THE FOREST OF ALASKA.

A sojourn in Alaska, without a compeer,
Hunting and trapping and chasing the deer;
Sheltered with comfort and plenty in store,
In a snug little cabin with ground for its floor.

On a bed of dry leaves my limbs find repose,
Proudly I wear my forest-made clothes;
A wealth of warm furs—pelts of my store—
Abound in the cabin with ground for its floor.

Smoke from my wigwam curls high in the air,
A pot of rich venison is steaming in there;
The latch-string hangs outside on the door
Of the neat little cabin with ground for its floor.

Welcome, ye nimrods—when the river you ford
Come to my shelter and feast at my board;
Three-legged stools stand "forninst" the door,
In the snug little cabin with ground for its floor.

Ye adorers of Nature, ye praising divines,
Come to the forest where your goddess reclines;
Here gaze upon scenes of grandeur in store,
Akin to that awaiting on the evergreen shore.

Alaska! imperial of mountain, glacier and braes,
All peerless in grandeur creation displays;
A land rescued from imperious reign,
A grand accession to Freedom's domain.

REUNION.

Come, old friends, join in a social day,
Father Time presses onward—we are old and gray;
In reunion we'll recall incidents of yore,
Revive old tales and rhymes—have greetings galore.

The recitations of youth—we'll repeat them anew,
As "fond recollection presents them to view";
We'll confirm early readings memory hath in store,
From "quaint and curious volumes of forgotten lore."

We'll open in meetly form with "Holy Willie's Prayer,"
Then Ichabod will Crane his neck to "Tam O'Shanter's mare";
That "Caesar had his Brutus"—how "Wallace bled" we'll tell,
And that "Freedom shrieked when Kosciusko fell."

We will "swim the Hellespont" and cross the "Bridge of Sighs,"
And dive "in the bosom of the deep where Holland lies";
We'll visit the cosy cottage whose smoke "so gracefully curls,"
And solve the knotty problem, "what to do with our girls."

"Auld Lang Syne" we'll sing, on "Sweet Home" we'll dwell,
And seize "the moss-covered bucket that hung in the well";
For the woodman to "spare that tree" we will implore,
And invoke that "hard times comes again no more."

In common "we hold these truths to be self-evident,"
That it is better to "be right than President";
That industrious habits should "in each bosom reign,"
And that "Truth crushed to earth shall rise again."

Bequeathed by Washington to endless fame,
Was the Starry Flag on land and ocean main;
A flag flaunting Liberty in repellent seas,
Proudly unfurled, "braves the battle and the breeze."

Bounteously are we allowed to "behold this joyous day,"
From "ignoble strife keep the noiseless tenor of your way";
The "cannon's opening roar" is frightful to be borne,
0, "Ye Ancient Mariners," "man was made to mourn."

"As we go marching on," "hand in hand we'll go,"
"We hear their gentle voices calling, our heads are bending low";
"Hold the fort! for we are coming," on the "Swiftsure Line,"
To dwell with him once living at "Bingen on the Rhine."

www.ingramcontent.com/pod-product-compliance
Lightning Source LLC
Chambersburg PA
CBHW070427010526
44118CB00014B/1939